BAPTISED AMONG CROCODILES

A history of the Daintree Aboriginal Mission 1940-1962

Russell Guy

First published in 1999 by the Assembly of God

Second published by:
Boolarong Press
655 Toohey Road
Salisbury Qld 4107
Australia
www.boolarongpress.com.au

National Library of Australia Cataloguing-in-Publication entry:

Creator:	Guy, Russell, author.
Title:	Baptised among crocodiles : a history of the Daintree Aboriginal Mission 1940-1962 / Russell Guy.
Edition:	2nd edition.
ISBN:	9781925236569 (paperback)
Subjects:	Hetherington, Isobella. Assembly of God (Daintree, Qld.) Daintree Aboriginal Mission. Missionaries--Queensland--Daintree Region. Kuku-Yalanji (Australian people)--Queensland--Daintree Region--History. Aboriginal Australians--Missions--Queensland--Daintree Region--History. Daintree Region (Qld.)
Dewey Number:	266.94943

Typeset in Adobe Caslon Pro 12pt.

Printed and bound by Watson Ferguson & Company, Salisbury, Brisbane, Australia.

CONTENTS

LIST OF ILLUSTRATIONS

ACKNOWLEDGEMENTS

The author wishes to thank the Mossman Assembly of God for interviews with the late Ps Jack Easton, Ps Jack Goulder and Leila Galliene (nee Cole) during the 'Back to Daintree' week in August 1995, and acknowledges the assistance of Ps Arthur and Elaine Westbrook, Lily and George Fischer, the late Jack Easton, Wilma Walker, the late Agnes Davidson, Mike and Wilma Meyer, Daphne Watkins, Alice Marbach, Lena Pitt, Lillian Westbrook, Norman Mitchell, Mrs Grace Crees, Laurie Boswell, Mr & Mrs Eddie Jenkins, Jack and Yvonne Goulder, Keith and Dawn Hannah, Mrs Marjorie Cope, Dawn Parker, Fred & Doris Lancaster, Clare O'Gilvie, Barry Chant, Stan Hunt, Billy Denman, Judy Shuan, Kathleen Myra Bogle, Ernest James Bogle and Gloria Neale AOG Qld State Clerk, Brisbane, Kathy Frankland and Margaret Reid at the Community and Personal History Section of the Department of Aboriginal and Torres Strait Island Policy and Development, Brisbane, staff at Mossman library, Kara Falls, James Cook University library, Cairns, T.A.F.E. library, Cairns, Australian Institute of Aboriginal and Torres Strait Islander Studies, Canberra, Professor Joseph Reser, JCU, Queensland Museum and Steven Stanley, Computer Support Technician, JCU, Cairns.

This is an historical account of culture contact between the Kuku-Yulanji of Mossman and Daintree, Christian missionaries, and government agents at the pentecostal Daintree Aboriginal Mission in North Queensland, Australia from 1940 to 1962. Some of the people interviewed and spoken about in this history have since passed away and care should be taken if read to members of community or family.

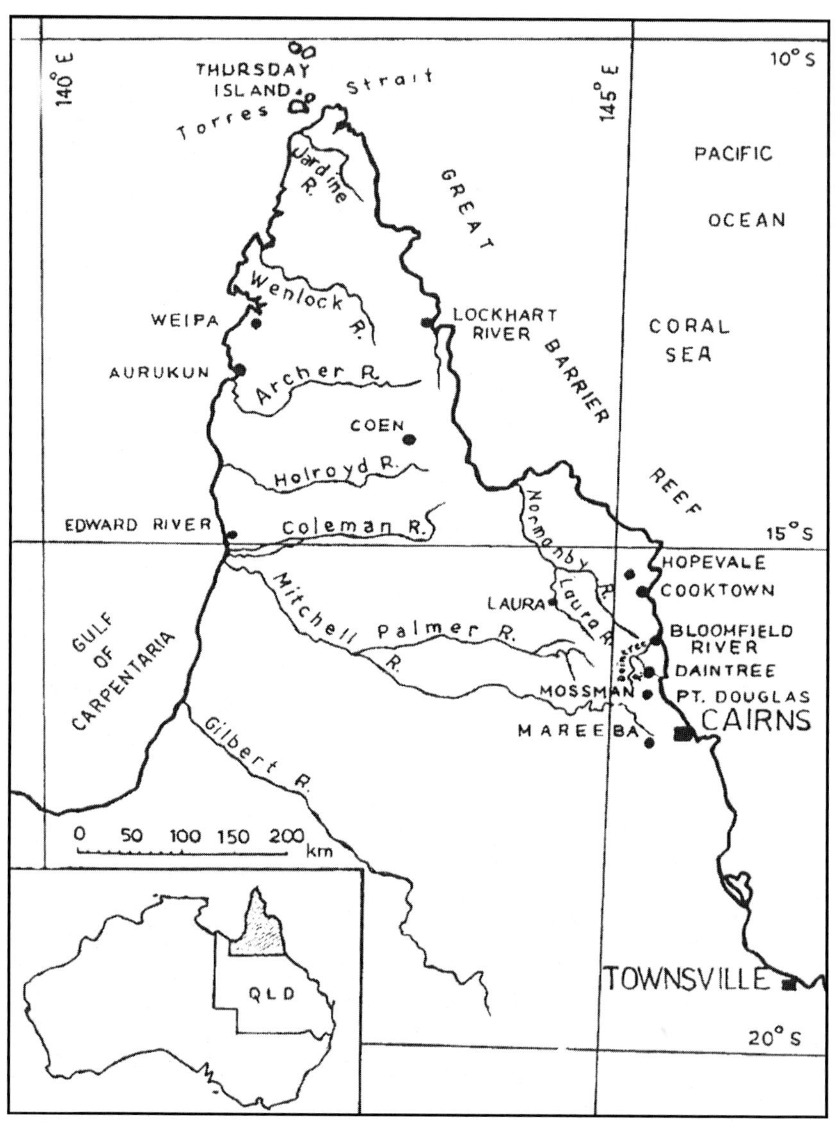

Illustration 2. Cape York, map cited in Anderson (1984).

CHAPTER ONE

EUROPEAN SETTLEMENT LEADING TO MISSIONARY ACTIVITY IN NORTH QUEENSLAND

In 1844, the New South Wales Legislative Council commissioned Ludwig Leichardt to survey an overland route north to Port Essington in the hope of discovering new grazing lands and establishing trade with Asia. Loos (1982) writes that in doing so Leichardt "dramatically brought the attention of the rest of Australia to the potential of North Queensland." Shortly after Leichardt's return, in December 1848, the thirty year old explorer Edmund Kennedy and his assistant, the Aboriginal, Jackey, were pushing through Cape York in north Queensland to the waiting supply ship at Albany Passage when a fatal spear lodged in Kennedy's back (Beale, 1970:207). The death of Kennedy was reported in the Sydney Morning Herald on 5 March, 1849. Bennett (1927:27) records that

> on the Barcoo, where no white man had been before him, Kennedy had found the natives friendly, but along the coast they were hostile, though in Flinders' time they had been well disposed. Since then they had suffered from raids, and one white man, as he sailed by the York Islands, shot at the blacks for practice, and recorded a successful hit in the book kept at Booby Island for the use of ships. Seeing the note an officer of

> the Beagle remarked - "I pity the first white man who comes within reach of that tribe."

In 1860, the year after Queensland had been proclaimed a colony, George Elphinstone Dalrymple, Commissioner for Crown Land, pioneered the first settlement north of Rockhampton at Bowen. He encountered Aboriginal resistance and gunfire ensued (Farnfield, 1968: 24). To increase the prosperity of the new colony, land was brokered abroad and within ten years, the Queensland population increased by fifty thousand. Investors believed that the new land laws might eventually allow for freehold title on pastoral leases, however, there were many 'run-jobbers' who claimed land purely for speculative purposes (Farnfield, 1968:14).

Massive public opposition forced the abandonment of convict transportation in 1849 and many former convicts now sought a future in the new colony. Harris (1990:238) notes "some of the most outspoken critics of frontier immorality were ex-convicts. There were also fair minded and moral people among the landowners." The depletion of water-holes by sheep and cattle, especially in drought conditions, was a major reason for the early conflict between Aborigines and Europeans (Erickson, 1970:37). The North Queensland historian Glenville Pike (1978:49) writes

> It was a long, unequal struggle that lasted throughout the period of the Queensland frontier - sixty years of massacre and counter-massacre.

DEVELOPING THE NORTH

In 1872, William Harm, commissioned by the Queensland government 'to explore Cape York Peninsula to assess its mineral and settlement potential', was the first to enter the Kuku-Yalanji traditional land - a cultural and linguistic boundary containing "a constellation of closely related dialect groups" (Wood, 1990:5) - which began just south of Cooktown and ended around the South Mossman River (Kerr 1979:2:21; Loos 1982:63; Anderson 1994:16). Included were the coastal mangrove swamps, much of what is today the Wet Tropics World Heritage Daintree rainforest and the drier country west to the Palmer River and Mt Carbine (Bamanga Bubu Ngadimunku, 1996:8; Roth,1899: QSA:19898). Frederick Warner, a member of Hann's party found gold on the Palmer River and this discovery created a dramatic change in the pace of northern development.

In 1873, Dalrymple received a government commission and arrived in the Daintree River, naming it after the former government geologist, Richard Daintree. He named the nearby Mossman River and noticed the wealth of red cedar (Farnfield, 1968:135; Neilsen, 1997:60). James Venture Mulligan opened up the Palmer River goldfield later that year (23) and almost overnight, Cook's Town, a sandalwood and beche de mer port which lay 116 miles east at the mouth of the Endeavour River, roared into life.

A contingent of Native Mounted Police, bearing the new breech-loading Snider rifles, arrived in Cook's Town with the first gold warden, Howard St George. Kirkman (1980:124) notes "considerable effort was expended by the Aborigines in attacks on property - cattle, horses and telegraph lines - thus exploiting the miner's chief enemy, isolation. . . . Disdaining conciliation, preferring retaliatory actions, the first wave of alluvial miners created a legacy of mutual hatred which was at the root of clashes throughout the late 1870s, the 1880s and even into the 1890s."

The Palmer River goldrush brought thousands of European and Chinese men to the area. In March 1874, a recent emigrant from England, George Wilcox arrived on the steamer 'Lichart' from Maryborough with two companions. They walked inland to the diggings but met with high food prices and starvation. Returning to Cooktown, "five months" after the rush had begun, Wilcox commented that although there were 5000 men, there was "no place of worship started yet." On May 10th, he wrote in his diary

> this was the first Sunday that any minister had been in Cooktown to hold any service and so we had an opportunity of going to hear him. The Church of England Service was read in the Police Station both morning and evening (4).

All records of births and deaths from the most northerly government post of Cardwell which had been established by Dalrymple in 1864, were now sent to Cook's Town (3). In 1873, Dalrymple had named Island Point, the headland on which Port Douglas now stands. There are reports that Europeans had been camped on the present-day site of Cairns from the 1860's (2), but it was Mulligan's discovery of gold on the Hodgkinson River in 1875 that put Cairns and Port Douglas on the map.

On the Mossman River, a Jamaican negro named Dan Hart (1817 -1900) was cutting cedar. These giants of the forest were rafted together and floated down the river to ships at sea. As it was with waterholes and gold, the depletion of timber was the cause of conflict. Hart had been attacked by an Aboriginal party the previous year, allegedly because some whitemen had taken a mummified body. Farnfield (1968:134) gives an account of Dalrymple's party removing a mummified body of a woman for shipment to the Brisbane Museum. Thomas Hanley, John Kegan and another were speared to death whilst cutting cedar along the banks of the Daintree River (7) as the Kuku-Yulanji became increasingly concerned by the millions of feet of cedar being taken out of the forest and the general sense that their domain was fast becoming untenable.

Land selection at Mossman, once known as Hartsville, was proclaimed by government gazette in March, 1877. The Port Douglas Historical society noted that 'land speculators were well aware of the importance of the potential "sugar lands" of the Mossman and Daintree River valleys and with the assistance of the Native Police, choice parcels along the streams were quickly taken up' (6). In 1885, Hart, who had planted the first cane on land which is now in the centre of Mossman, found himself surrounded by settlers cultivating sugar cane. One of those was of Sydney Algernon Barnard, who arrived from Melbourne in 1883 at the age of 21. Neglecting the warning to go armed at all times Barnard "was speared by natives in March 1885, in retaliation for the deeds of others" (Kerr, 1979). It is alleged that a punitive expedition followed, led "by the local police inspector and his native troopers. The full tribe was cornered in a gully. The only survivor, a little baby" (Franken, 1964). Barnard was buried in the Port Douglas cemetery below the inscription "...killed by the blacks on the Mossman River. 'Watch therefore! For ye know neither the day nor hour, wherein the Son of Man cometh! (Matthew 25.13)'."

In April, 1877, in response to demand for a road to service the mining outposts opening up south of Cooktown, Christie Palmerston and William Lakeland, probed the eucalypt forest of the main coastal range and descended a long spur, following an Aboriginal walking track down into the Mowbray valley. On 11 June, 1877 at Thornborough, over 200 pounds was subscribed at a public meeting to reward Palmerston and Lakeland (Johnston, 1986; Lloyd, 1997). Later that month, the 'S.S. Corea', Captained by D. H. Owen and chartered by Cooktown businessmen, anchored off Island Point which was renamed Port Owens. Residents of Cairns and Smithfield quickly heard about the new anchorage and came north aboard the cutter 'Fairy', Mr Ingham's steam launch 'Fitzroy' and the ketch 'Terrigal'. They renamed Island Point, Port Salisbury. Pioneers and teamsters turned Palmerston's track into a rough cutting servicing the inland mining settlements. This was one of the first roads in north Queensland and it became known as 'the Bump'.

In November, the Colonial Treasurer, J. R. Dickson visited Port Salisbury, proclaiming it a Port of Entry for the warehousing of dutiable goods. It quickly becoming a major port for trade and passengers sailing between Melbourne and England, as well as disembarking South Sea Islanders, principally Melanesian, 'Kanak' labourers (Johnston, 1986; Lloyd, 1997). Approximately 62,000 were indentured as labourers for the South West Pacific labour trade between 1863 -1904 (Docker, 1970; Farnfield, 1968). A Police Sergeant was appointed in December 1877, and the force grew to thirty, including a detachment of twenty native troopers. A hospital began (8) and Port Salisbury was re-named Port Douglas after the premier of Queensland.

The Chinese goldminers now an integral part of the community, built temples, ('Joss' houses), in Cooktown, Port Douglas and Cairns (10). There was considerable enmity towards the Chinese miners which culminated in legislation known as the White Australia policy (Pike, 1978:289). Lloyd (1994) notes that the Chinese were

> lessees or tenants... growing maize, coffee, bananas, fruits and large tracts of rice. When some became successful cane growers there was much hostility, as there had been on the goldfields.

Tin was found at Herberton and on Waterfall Creek near Cooktown in 1878 (9). On the Daintree River, a small settlement flourished in the wake of pioneers such as John

Stewart, Heinrich Fischer and Frank Osbourne who took up land in 1881. Jack Shewan was an early cedar getter in the area and many Aboriginal people bear the Shewan and Fischer name today. In the 1880s, the Niau family who had originally come from France as part of a contingent of Colonists, settled on the Daintree. In the 'The Phantom Paradise', Josephine Niau says that her father had attempted to grow sugarcane on

> two square miles of valuable timber country, with two miles of river frontage. The sale of timber brought a goodly sum, but there was little profit by the time roads were made through the jungle and teamsters were paid to bring their bullocks to drag the heavy logs to the river. . . . The flooding of the English market with beet-sugar killed all prospect of the erection of the (promised) mill on the Daintree River. . . . Where the cane had formerly waved, my father grew maize for the market. Bush-fires burnt the first crop - floods completely ruined the second. Our little family, one after the other, fell sick of fever. (Niau, 1936:184-5).

The demand for red cedar continued throughout the 1880s, but by 1888, it was completely cut-out (12) and John (Jack) Shewan turned to dairying. In 1891, the Cairns to Kuranda railway opened, quickly becoming the favoured inland access and traffic on the arduous 'Bump' track declined as did the prospects for Port Douglas.

THE PROSPECTS FOR KUKU-YALANJI IN THE DAINTREE

As the European presence in the North increased, Christian churches and missionaries began to have an influence. There were missionaries as far north as Somerset on northern Cape York in 1867, as well as mission initiatives at Weipa and on government reserves at Cooktown and Yarrabah, near Cairns.

In 1896, Archibald Meston, commissioned by the government, noted that "the 'town-blacks everywhere are in a demoralised condition, from Brisbane to Cooktown" (Meston, 1896:7). Missionaries and Aboriginal Protector Dr. Roth were dismayed over the heavy death rate among Aboriginal people addicted to opium. Opium was available in exchange for work and sexual services (Haviland 1980:134). Even the police found it impossible to control, but were unable to persuade the government to surrender the 30,000 pounds per annum opium import revenue (Haviland, 1980:134). Opium was a dutiable item and readily available in several stores in Port Douglas until about 1907 (Kerr, 1979).

At the height of the Palmer River goldrush, the government allocated money for the establishment of Aboriginal reserves, which were "Crown land under another name" (D. Thompson, 1996:157) and "generally reduced in size as the towns grew" (Loos 1988:102). The state provided support to various churches who had established missions by providing land and financial assistance (1). However financial assistance declined after 1893. Meston (1896: 7) wrote that the total expense at the two Cape Bedford missions near Cooktown had been borne "for three years... by a religious society in Germany, an act of unselfish generosity prompted evidently by no other motive than religious zeal and philanthropy."

The situation at Bloomfield, a Lutheran mission situated in a valley between Cooktown and the Daintree, "on a Kuku-Yalanji clan estate - Wujalwujal" (Anderson 1988:327), and therefore remote, was vastly different to those at Cape Bedford. As was so often the case, the character of the missionary was crucial. Some succeeded where others failed, and pressures were "many and diverse" but Aboriginal residents were free to come and go (Anderson, 1988:326-327).

Anderson (1988:328-331) notes

> with the power that accrued from being able to live on one's own estate, and knowing the resources and advantages provided by having resident Europeans, it is not surprising that Aborigines from nearby estates tried to urge the missionaries to come to their country... the mission was exploited as a depot for rations and implements. ... It seems also that Aboriginal parents used the mission to protect their daughters against the abuses of local European men. It was almost certainly also used generally by some Bloomfield Aborigines as a refuge against depredations and revenge killings by other Aborigines.

A different situation existed at Yarrabah, sited across the inlet from Cairns. Loos (1988:112) writes that from 1895 the Anglican missionary at Yarrabah, Rev Ernest Gribble

> was especially motivated by the plight of Aboriginal children in the camps (around settled areas in North Queensland). They were frequently orphaned, starving, or diseased... addicted to alcohol or opium... becoming prostitutes.... Gribble's intense passion for rescuing destitute children was largely responsible for the speed with which the permanent mission community grew.

In 1899, Protector Roth (1900:7) noted that the Yarrabah Mission school included lectures on opium and alcohol which resulted in a number of senior Aboriginal men forming a governing body to combat the mis-use of these substances. One of the first measures the governing body instituted was suppression of opium within the mission reserve. From 1900, Yarrabah began printing its own 'Aboriginal News', had "six farms, all fully managed by Aborigines and Islanders", a fire brigade, rifle corps and brass band, a court and nine outstations connected by "an old" telephone system presented by the New South Wales government {Higgins, 1981:11).

Despite co-operation between missionaries and Aborigines, there was often antipathy between Queensland government officials and missionaries. Home Secretary Tozer informed the Queensland parliament in 1897 "although some assert that religion has a civilizing influence on the blacks… I would not advise the state to incur one single farthing of expense in anything but the secular education of the blacks" (Harrison, 1990: 37). Tozer had the year before received Meston's report which stated

> the advent of the whites, and the too prevalent discord between the two races, has in many places created mutual friendship between tribes originally hostile, and broken down the old exclusive tribal barriers… the old order of things is passing away, and they must adapt themselves to the changed environment, just as white races, individuals and communities, have to adapt themselves to sudden or gradual changes all over the face of the earth. Their land has been taken from them on no other title than the law of the strongest, and they must make the best of any alternative the strongest chooses to offer (Meston, 1896:9).

THE TWENTIETH CENTURY

After the failure of a sugar mill at Bloomfield and the prospects at Daintree, pioneers and settlers banded together and mortgaged their land back to the government in return for finance to erect a mill at Mossman. A company was formed in December, 1894 and Mossman was recognised as a settlement in 1896. Meston (1896:10) noted the 1885 massacre in which "the Mossman blacks have been exterminated, but the old Port Douglas tribe (Chabbuki) and a few of the Mowbray River blacks are camped a short distance along the beach from Port Douglas". Meston's use of 'Chabbuki' corresponds to the present day term of Tjapukai which is the language used by the group, including sub-group dialects, occupying the narrow coastal strip south to Port Douglas (Wood; 1990:5).

The Mossman mill crushed its first cane in 1897, the year Queensland government legislated the 'Aboriginals Protection and the Restriction of the Sale of Opium Act.' This was the first comprehensive Aboriginal protection and segregation Act in Australia, effectively making Aborigines wards of the state. With the consequent loss of hunting grounds, starvation was recognised as a factor in Aboriginal attacks on cattle, crops and stores. The fact that Aboriginal people were hemmed in and continually harassed by the Native Police, caused the Police Commissioner to inform the government that it was "necessary to protect the Aborigines from starvation" (15). Evans (1969:14) notes

> the chief means of 'taming' the Aborigines and thus protecting live-stock, was the Native Police. Their brutality is undoubted, surprise attacks would result in the slaughter of many women, children and old men. The Irvinebank case of 1884 was typical of this. The Native Police often 'cleared' an area by forcing the Aborigines to relinquish their land and move beyond the limits of settlement.

The Native Police could not use their open country tactics in the rainforests of North Queensland. Hunter et al. (1999:50) note "the Native Police killed an estimated 5000 Aboriginal people in the process of 'dispersal' and frontier justice between 1849 and 1897." Settlers on the Atherton Tableland advocated rationing, which ran counter to Native Police deployment, although a detachment was currently being formed on the Mossman River. The government was urged to start a mission station or reserve to pacify the problem which was holding up development in the area. Meston (1896: 10) recommended Charles Masterton, a Daintree selector as "a man of integrity and an old and trusted friend of the aboriginals" to be deputised for the weekly distribution of rations via the Port Douglas cutter, a 30ft boat built and operated by the Osbourne family. Loos (1982:116) writes

> the dramatic success of the experiment to control frontier resistance by rationing depended on the willingness of the Aborigines to accept such a scheme. An important incentive for the Aborigines seems to have been their inability to meet their kinship obligations adequately in conditions of frontier conflict, especially with regard to support of the aged members of the tribe.

Implementing this new policy, after years of massacre and dispersal, Aboriginal Protectors (now the local police Sergeant) reporting to the Chief Protector (the Police Commissioner from 1901), had the power to remove Aboriginal people from their communities. The Protector controlled an Aboriginal person's right to marry a non-Aboriginal person, distributed government rations, issued permits and apportioned the nett amount of wages.(Section 13 of the 1901 amendments gave the Protector the right to manage all property belonging to an Aboriginal person.)

The Pacific Island Labourers Act of 1901 forced many thousands of Sea Islanders to be deported, but approximately 2500 remained, and on Sundays many of them visited various Mission churches. The Queensland sugar industry had depended on South Sea Island labour, but in 1898, Japanese labour was imported to the Far North Queensland cane fields. When they went on strike, Indian labourers were called in, mixing with "time expired" Kanakas and Chinamen, and eventually the South Sea Islanders left the industry (36).

In July 1901, the Mossman Central Mill Company changed its articles to prevent any Chinaman or Asiatic from acquiring shares in the Company through mortgaging their deed of land. By 1908, the White Australian policy was established, deporting many Chinese and Kanakas, and the Company deleted the clause from their articles. As restricted numbers of Italian labourers arrived to cut cane, the Bishop of North Queensland, George Frodsham spoke at the Church of England's 1906 Australian Congress in Melbourne

> We have an airy way of speaking about Australia being a white man's country. But Australia first of all was a black man's country and I have never heard that a black man invited us to take his property away from him.
>
> A previous speaker at this Congress has said that the 'British were put by God into Australia to preach the gospel to the heathen.' I have never heard a more complete condemnation of the stewardship of the Australian people. We have developed the country and we have civilised it, but we have certainly done very little to preach the gospel to the people we have dispossessed. The blacks have been shot and poisoned while they were wild and dangerous. They are now left to kill themselves with white vices where they have been 'tamed,' but very few have received at our hands either justice or consideration (Harris, 1990:699).

Twenty five miles north of Mossman, on the Daintree River, Harry Fischer imported a Brahman bull from Melbourne Zoo and realising the advantage of hardy tropical cattle, began to build up a herd. On St Patrick's Day, 1911, Port Douglas was all but destroyed by a cyclone which claimed the lives of two men. The cyclone flattened buildings in the town and many were not rebuilt.

In 1916, during the 1914 - 1918 War (16), the Mossman Gorge was gazetted a Government Reserve comprising 64 acres. A pioneer cane farmer named J. D. (Jack) Johnson of Mango Park Estate, brother to the freehold owner of neighbouring 'Drumsara', donated the land and insisted that it be made a reserve for the local Aboriginal community (17).

Aboriginal wages were levied for welfare on government reserves. By the early 1920's, Italian labourers were coming into the cane growing districts in increasing numbers. The Port Douglas Post Office, Court House and banks re-sited to Mossman, and Port Douglas as a major port and trading centre declined (18).

Around this time, a missionary who was to have an influence in the beginning of the Mossman and Daintree missions, Isabella Hetherington, a nursing sister who gained passage to Australia by tending to an invalid on board ship, (19) was making plans to travel to travel north. Hetherington, born in Ireland in 1871 of landholding parents who came out of the first stirrings of the Welsh Revival, part of the late-nineteenth century Pentecostal movement to work among Aboriginal people (20). She was thirty two years old when she arrived in Australia on 24 December, 1903 and settled in Ballarat, Victoria. Hetherington began two years of missionary work among Aboriginal people on the banks of the Murray River, before joining the Aboriginal Mission and serving three years in Wellington, N.S.W.

Some say that she proceeded to La Perouse, just south of Sydney on the shores of Botany Bay (21) where it was that she acquired a life-long companion in a young Aboriginal girl named Nellie. The historian Barry Chant (1998) writes that Hetherington met Nellie in Wellington and that she may have been asked to take the young Aboriginal girl and educate her as a dying request from the child's mother. In 1912, she settled on a small Aboriginal reserve with fifty inhabitants near Port MacLeay in South Australia (Chant, 1998) where she met the Swiss immigrant and missionary, Ernest Kramer, married to Effie Buchanan, sister of W.A Buchanan, a pioneer of the Pentecostal movement in Australia. The Kramers offered to join her in Aboriginal ministry.

It is known that Hetherington was baptising on an Aboriginal mission at Bunyip, Victoria, in 1923 (Chant 1973: 49) (22), that she was in Maryborough, southern Queensland, in 1928 where Nellie sang for the newly formed Christian mission and later led a crusade on the western Queensland streets of Cloncurry. There is some dispute about the year of her arrival in Mossman. It could have been in the late 1920's (22) but may have been 1930 (23). From the late-1920s, a number of Aboriginal, feminist, church and other organisations were agitating for Aboriginal land and citizenship rights (Lake 1997). When Hetherington arrived in Mossman, the Kuku-Yulanji were in several camps, dependent on traditional foods and the rations of the Protector, among whose duties fell the task of removing children of mixed descent, policing the reserves at Mossman and Daintree and reporting on the activities of missionaries.

ENDNOTES

1. A guide to Queensland Government records relating to Aboriginal; Torres Strait Islander peoples. Volume 1. Published by the Queensland State Archives and the Dept. of Family Services and Aboriginal and Islander Affairs. Brisbane. 1994.
2. Claude Leroy interview with author. Cairns. 15/5/96. Spinifex & Wattle 1903 -1905. R. A. Johnson, 1984:2.
3. Leroy maintains that in 1932, his friend and local carrier, Clevie J Solomon was paid one pound sterling per day by the Cooktown Shire Council to take all the records to the dump.
4. Diary of George Wilcox. Port Douglas Historical Society Inc. 1997.
5. Douglas Shire Historical Society Inc. Museum display
6. 'Daintree's Early Years, pub. Daintree School. 1988.
7. Mossman Hospital: our first fifty years. 1980. Mossman Hospitals

Board

8. Leroy. Personal conversation.
9. 'A Joss House, Lit Sung Goong, was built in Cairns 1887. Worshippers were from the Chung San district in China. The temple was used for more than a place of religious significance. It was a focal point of community life.' Rotary Club of Cairns Bicentennial plaque at 93A Grafton St., Cairns. Pike describes the services offered by the Chinese to the Diggers on the field and in Cooktown: "Both Cairns and Darwin owed the Chinese a debt in the struggling early days."
10. The mission was abandoned and its reserve status revoked in 1902, but the Kuku-Yalanji residents remained. It was re-established in 1957, but drastically reduced in size. Source: Qld State Archives & Dept. of Family Services and Aboriginal and Islander Affairs. Records Guide. Vol. 2.
11. Daintree's Early Years, pub. Daintree School. 1988.
12. Early Days of the Douglas Shire. Keith and Valda Prince. 1977. Mossman: Douglas Shire Council.
13. Mossman Gazette. 2/10/97. p. 10.
14. Report of the Commissioner for Police for 1878', 1879 Votes & Proceeding of the Queensland Parliament, p. 752.
15. Of the 145 who had enlisted from within the Douglas Shire, 39 were killed in action. Returned servicemen and women, some of whom were Aboriginal were awarded small selections, known as a soldier settler's block; but it is not known if any were Kuku-Yalanji. George Kennedy, a Wiradjuri was awarded a block near Ivanhoe, N.S.W. after service with the 6th Light Horse Regiment in Egypt, France and England. Aust. 14/5/96. The 3rd, 8th and 10th Light Horse were decimated at Gallipoli in 1915.
16. (Ernest) Bogle interviewed by author. Mossman. June 1996.
17. Mossman Hospital: our first fifty years. 1980. Mossman Hospitals Board.
18. Agnes Davidson. Interview. Toowoomba Retirement Village.
19. Ps Arthur Westbrook. Interview at Mossman. Oct. 1995.

20. Kathleen Myra Bogle interview with author. Cairns. July 1997.

21. Information relating to Sister Hetherington's work at Good News Hall - personal conversation with Barry Chant 11/3/96 and Qld State Archives A/58838 letter no. 40/1820. A letter sent to the Chief Protector of Aborigines in the State of Queensland by Herbert R. Drake of Ballarat East, in July 1940, records that the author ministered with Sister I. Hetherington to Aborigines in Victoria seventeen years ago. Considering the accuracy of this information, the year was 1923.

22. Queensland State Archives. File 6Q/7 13/2/48.

23. Inscribed on gravestone at Mt Molloy cemetery: 'James Venture Mulligan. 1837-1907. Born Rothfriland, County Down. Migrated in 1860, found Palmer River gold in 1875, Hodgkinson river gold in 1875 which led to the establishment of Cairns and Port Douglas. He mined copper a Mt Molloy in the 1890s, married in 1903, bought the Mt Molloy hotel in 1905 and died on 24.8.1907 from injuries received when he tried to break up a fight in his hotel. He had no children.' According to Glenville Pike (Northern Frontier) Mulligan's autobiography was published in the Queenslander, 1904.

Illustration 3. 'Cutting steps with a tomahawk', photograph taken by Government Protector, Dr Roth, in the Cooktown area 1899.

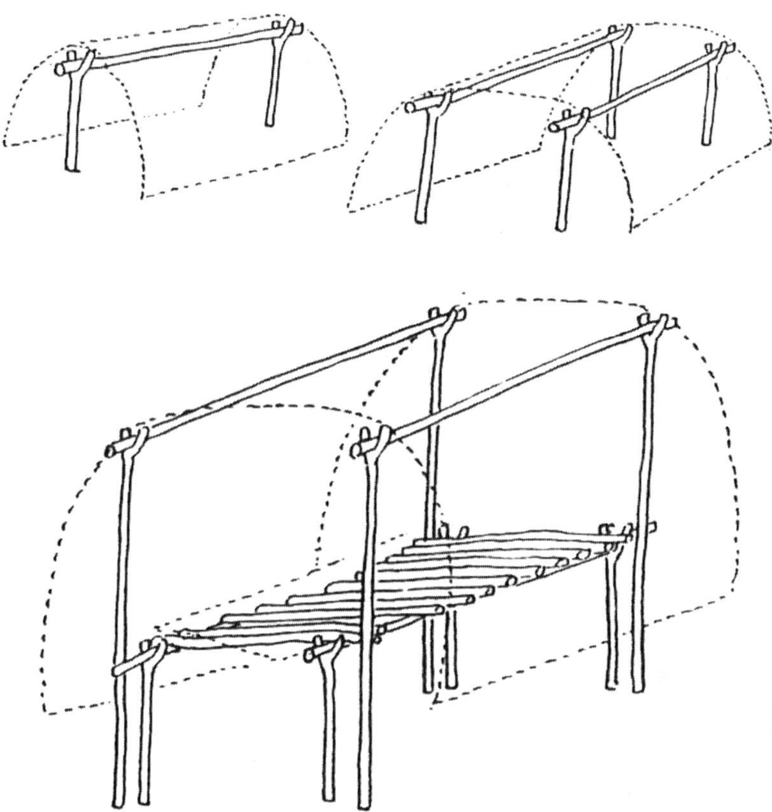

Illustration 4. "Sleeping Accommodation. The materials of which these Kokominni cover their huts are tea-tree, messmate, iron-bark or box-wood bark … Only occasionally do these blacks sleep on the ground … The more usual method, especially during the wet season, is to make use of a bunk, this being formed by short transverse sticks lying on the cross-pieces and covered with sheets of bark so as to make them more comfortable to lie upon.' Protector Roth's drawings near Cooktown, 1899.

CHAPTER TWO

1930–1940: MISSIONARIES ON THE MOSSMAN AND DAINTREE

Mossman Gorge is approximately two miles west of Mossman, nestled at the foot of a mountain known as Manjal Dimbi, which has its own 'story' in relation to Kuku-Yalanji religious belief (Bamanga Bubu Ngadimunku 1996:19). In pre-contact times, the Kuku-Yalanji subsisted by preparing rainforest fruit and plants (nutritional and medicinal) capturing scrub turkey, fish, honey, possum, eggs, tree kangaroo, fresh water shrimp, eel and seafood such as mud-whelks, turtle eggs, 'pipi' and fish etc. Anderson (1984:80) has written on the political and economic basis of Kuku-Yalanji social history

> the environment… was not, in a sense, an objective entity, fixed in nature and external to human life. Environment was a 'culturised', humanised landscape termed bubu, or 'country'. It was often described in human terms; changes in it were interpreted as changes in the human or social world. It was interacted with: spoken to and acted upon. In turn it re-acted by providing goods and resources or by withholding them and bringing hardship or climatic catastrophe upon humans (cf. Rigsby 1980:91).

Despite the punitive raid which followed Sydney Algernon Barnard's spearing on the banks of the Mossman River in 1885 (Kerr, 1979) and the claim that the "full tribe was cornered in a gully" and "exterminated" (Meston,1896: 10), religious beliefs survived in the large and itinerated Kuku-Yalanji tribal area (Neilsen, 1997:54; Wood, 1990:9). The Kuku-Yalanji were wards of state legislation when Sister Hetherington arrived in the small town which had a 'photoplay' moving picture theatre among the civic buildings clustered around the sugar mill.

Hetherington's party included Lizzy and Nellie, two Aboriginal women and a woman named Ethel Vale. According to Kathleen Myra Bogle who worked with Hetherington, Lizzy was from La Perouse. "Nellie's mother was dying and said to Sister Hetherington, 'take this baby and nurse her for me'. She brought her up, educated her and she learnt music. She sang in every town hall." Bogle first met Hetherington in "1929/30. She came to Rocky Point and we were living there in 1929. She had a meeting at our house. I was still 16. That's when I gave my life to the Lord and dedicated myself to mission work."

At first, Hetherington, a trained nurse who had spent ten years in a doctor's surgery (Vale, 1948), found accommodation in the town and walked around visiting camps, holding a service on Sunday and teaching rudimentary English. Her favourite Sunday dress was a long black dress, a couple of inches off the ground and her long white hair was specked with brown. She spoke with a thick brogue and was sixty-one years of age (1).

Wilma Walker, a Kuku-Yalanji resident of Mossman, was born at the Gorge. Her mother, a Kuku-Yalanji woman, born at Buru (China Camp), north of the Daintree, became known as Jessie Buchanan because she worked for Mrs Buchanan, a pioneer and owner of the Post Office Hotel in Mill St. Wilma's father, known as Barlow, who lived at Diamond Camp - Brie Brie - south Mossman where the cemetery is today, worked on a sugar farm nearby. Walker describes her first meeting with Hetherington.

> When Sister Hetherington first came to the Gorge people had no clothes on. My brother-in-law, Barney Lunn was going with my sister and he told the people in language to get ready because that lady was coming along with some clothes for them. Some of the people was frightened when Sister Hetherington came, but Barney talked all the time. They called him Barney Lunn because he worked for Mr Lunn. Mr Lunn used to come here for Barney to go with him to do mowing and gardening. Then Mr Lunn was selling cars. Barney was born at the Gorge. He help everyone and could speak a little bit of English. The people didn't want him [Sister Hetherington] to live there, but people liked him [sic] 'cause he was a kind lady. She helped the people. The people were good, not smoking or drinking.
>
> She came with Nellie from somewhere south. When they first came, they had black dress like nun clothes. They used to walk from Mossman to the Gorge and go up the Gorge looking for people.

Dalrymple made an observation about the nakedness of Kuku-Yalanji on the shore near Daintree in 1873 (Nielsen, 1997:53).

Kathleen Myra Bogle was born at Brie Brie on her parents small cane farm. Her mother and maternal grandfather who worked the Palmer River goldfield, were Hungarian. Her father, George Edgar Davis was born in Cooktown. His father George Snr., was an Irishman who was a member of the Cooktown Council and his mother was a part Aboriginal woman. Their son, George Edgar Davis, Kathleen's father, grew up at the Anglican mission at Yarrabah, became an altar boy and a deacon and learnt to play the pipe organ. He played in churches in Townsville and Charters Towers, in brass bands and sang Soprano in choirs. He was among those who started the

'Aboriginal News' at Yarrabah and later worked as a typesetter at the Cairns Post. Bogle remembers

> before Dad left Yarrabah, he was appointed as a Magistrate. He'd sit there in a Kangaroo Court. One time, a little boy who was hungry stole some bread. The word got back to the Superintendent and that little boy had to go before the court. They punished him by shaving his head and wrote on a placard, "I am a thief." Dad said he never forgot that.

After returning to Mossman in 1911 at the age of 21, Davis obtained farm work as a ploughman with Mr Crawford and Mr Muntz at Brie Brie to support his wife Caroline Rose and their first-born, Leonard. The next year, they started a small farm at Brie Brie and Kathleen was born, a twin to brother Charles. Kanakas from the New Hebrides were working in the Mossman fields.

The Davis family had Aboriginal descent from George's mother (Kathleen's grandmother) and worked their own farm. George had a Mission education and had been a musician and a typesetter. Barney Lunn could speak "a little bit of english" and did mowing and gardening for Mr Lunn, but lived at the Gorge.

Daintree, approximately 25 miles north, was isolated from Mossman and Port Douglas except by sea, where brothers Arthur and Chappie Osbourne ran the weekly mail run to Port Douglas. The Daintree River Development Company, formed to promote the timber and dairy industry in the late nineteenth century, built a butter factory, manager's residence, sawmill and Osbourne's grocery store in 1924. A school was erected the following year. Cattle grazing was well established (3). Entertainment was supplied by house parties at various farmers homes, dances at the butter factory or school and movies shown in the single men's hashhouse. The Aboriginal population "loved this and were the most enthusiastic patrons." (3). All around, scrub was being cleared and timber felled. A few miles upstream, an Aboriginal reserve, gazetted in 1926 (4) on an extremely steep hillside, dropped almost perpendicular to the river which, after a cyclone in 1927, was in flood.

A joint Aboriginal/European history of the Mossman and Daintree Kuku-Yalanji, 'JAKALBAKU' (5) describes the Aboriginal situation at the time

> as the land was taken up, the Aboriginals of the area were slowly forced to move from one area to another but never finding rest for very long. Dick Fischer (1902 - 1995), was born at a place called JIBA-JIBA (Dry River) on the Daintree River. He says, "At last they were bunched up and camping at JULAY (upriver from the present town of Daintree). George Kulka came down from China Camp about then and stayed, but then we shifted again up river some more on the same side. A lot of people buried over there."

The Government surveyed about 100 acres off for an Aboriginal reserve, quite near to where they were camping then, but the land was all steep ridge running down to the river and not much flat country, totally unsuitable for accommodating this large number of people.

Kathleen Bogle remembers Hetherington's early forays into the Daintree area around 1930

> I was part of her team. We used to spread a big tent, a bit out of Daintree town and have a campfire, a piano accordion and guitar. We sang Gospel songs for the first two nights. The people, mostly Aboriginal but some farmers and all that from Daintree, they loved it. The Martin family, the Willis, the Cobbs, the Fischers. They liked sing-along. They enjoyed it and were happy. On the third night, they're gonna get it because she's going to preach. Then they can make up their own minds if they're going to be baptised on the fourth day.

> Some would come to the baptism at a spot where little streams were running into the main Daintree river. It was full of crocodiles of course, but they'd walk in up to their waists, two Sisters. I was praying. Sister would say, "let's pray!" I was looking out for crocodiles.

A track led north from Mossman to Daintree via a bridge over Barrett's Creek which had been built in 1929. Daisy Smith was a pioneer missionary in the area at the time with another woman named Green. Daisy Smith's experiences were later recorded in The Australian Evangel and Glad Tidings Messenger (Oct. 1939)

> Many difficulties confront the work here, the nature of which it would be difficult to explain in detail. We are living in a tent 12ft by 12ft, on Mr P's property. They are very kind with their provisions of milk and vegetables and, when they kill, any amount of meat. Thus our God is providing for us in a marvellous way and we are happy in His loving care, waiting until our work begins in earnest. Then our days will be fully occupied in teaching and training the natives. Our first work will be to build a place for a school for the children. The aboriginals are busy getting wood for posts and uprights and we have a number of bags which we will sew together for sides. Then, for the roof we hope to have iron, so that bye and bye when we get a permanent school building, we shall be able to use it as a shelter for ourselves from the torrential tropical rains.
>
> We do praise God that to date the rains have been stayed, for it would be rather unpleasant in a tent under such circumstances, and with an open-air fire-place. At first, our 'bush-beds' were very hard; Sister Green's bed is covered with a cow hide. She says she has only slept on a bush bed ever since coming here, "but we are very happy".
>
> The coloured men are scrub-cutting in readiness for a garden, and although it is nearly too late for vegetables, we are going to plant paw paws, bananas, pineapples, beans, tomatoes, and other

> things that grow quickly and easily. We must teach the men to grow their own food.

Smith and Green were several miles upstream from Daintree while Hetherington concentrated her work at Mossman Gorge. A resident of the Gorge Kuku-Yalanji community, the late Eileen MacNamara describes the conditions

> Sometimes when there was a big fight, up she would run right out into the middle of the fight area and stop them. No one game to throw spear when she out there. Old Miss Hetherington would try to teach us some school, and the old people some English. I suppose I was an older teenager when we were shifted up river to where we are now. They wanted our camp site for cane. They came one day and pack us all up and walk us up the river. No road then, only old track. Miss Hetherington she help us get settled in and she start to build a humpy for herself, she started to live with us then and look after us. Most men working on cane now and we got a little school, sort of, run by Miss Hetherington. She bring medicine and stuff for our babies and children, this was good because not so many dying now, not like before. Sometime we would walk right down river to the beach and hunt fish, stay overnight and walk back. Police would come every Friday with rations and stuff for us, they'd come up and call your name then hand out the flour - sugar - tea - bully beef. Old Man Baldy, he got a bit cheeky one day and the police catch him swearing and he been sent to Palm Island. Never seen again, maybe he died there, I dunno! My mum used to work hard - scrub floors - washing clothes on an old wash board -sometime mind the children maybe. They give us bread, tea leaf, sugar, maybe, something to take home (7).

Erbacher (1991) records the Kuku-Yalanji tradition of 'Walmbaji-Peacemaker'

> as the name suggests, the peacemaker is there to restore peace when fighting breaks out within the tribe. The peacemaker

> stands between the opposing parties and will stop the fight. If a man has lost a fight and is going to kill himself because of his loss of face, the peacemaker will intervene. If someone threatens to kill another person the peacemaker will step in and restrain them. No one loses face, as they have been prevented from carrying out the killing. The peacemaker is much respected and when he enters into a conflict nobody dares cause him injury or disobey him.

Hetherington's actions in stopping the fight may have been observed as imitating the Walmbaji tradition, causing some Kuku-Yalanji to contemplate that their respective religious beliefs had a commonality. It is known that Kuku-Yalanji women used their digging sticks to deflect spears between opposing parties (7). The new Mossman hospital was opened on the Gorge road on 23rd August, 1930 and subsequent photographs show Aboriginal people in the care of nursing staff. Hetherington would have had to liase with the Police Protector as the Kuku-Yulanji were moved off their camp at the mouth of the Mossman River and concentrated at the Mossman Gorge Reserve.

In March 1932, Hetherington was asked to preach in the 'Canvas Cathedral', 1200 miles south at Brisbane. There was no road between Mossman and Cairns, so with Nellie accompanying her, the two women would have had to either take the boat from Port Douglas or a buggy up the Bump track and across the Tablelands to the Kuranda rail terminal. The Canvas Cathedral was part of a Revival Crusade led by William Booth-Clibborn, an American born, Pentecostal evangelist and the grandson of General William Booth, who founded the Salvation Army in 1878. (8). Booth-Clibborn came to Australia in the early 1930's, first to Melbourne and New South Wales and then to Queensland. He came up to Rockhampton before stationing himself in Barry Parade,

Fortitude Valley, Brisbane, where the Canvas Cathedral, a big marquee, was erected opposite to where the Glad Tidings Tabernacle now stands. The Evangel (March 1931) reported that it was 'the greatest religious revival Brisbane has seen.' (9)

In the audience that night in 1932, was a young man named Jack Easton, who was to become a Daintree missionary in 1945. "When she preached the Word, the Holy Spirit spoke to my heart and I'm a product of her. Quickened by the Spirit. That's what it is. She had Nellie with her. They called her Nellie Hetherington and she had a good singing voice. Nell used to sing solos." Nellie sang 'The Hope of the Aboriginals' (Chant, 1998:7).

THE HOPE OF THE ABORIGINALS

Stan Hunt's history of the formation of the Assembly of God (AOG) in Australia (Hunt, 1978) identifies Sister Hetherington as having attended the conference of the AOG in Rockhampton the following year

> there was a woman at that conference who was to lead the church into a lasting mission to the Aborigines. Isabel(la) Hetherington, a missionary from Northern Ireland, had spent 29 years ministering to the Aborigines, including a faith mission in the Mossman area of North Queensland since 1926.
>
> Apparently, she came to the Assemblies of God for assistance, for she spoke of her experience and told the conference about the neglected condition of the Aborigines. Her speech must have been convincing, because she set in motion towards a mission in the Mossman - Daintree district (10).

Stan Hunt and Kathleen Bogle both list Hetherington's arrival in Mossman as earlier than 1930. Hunt gives 1926 and Bogle indicates that she first met her in "1929/30. She might have been in Mossman a couple of years before I met her. She said she wasn't well known there." Ethel Vale, in her 1948 letter to the Director of Native Affairs said that she arrived in 1930. Therefore, it is not certain that after being in Mossman about six years and the local Protector suggesting that Hetherington move onto the Reserve as Vale's letter states, that the year was 1930. It may have been a few years earlier.

A road connecting Cairns, Mossman and Daintree was built in 1933. Around this time, Sister Hetherington, Nellie, Ms Vale and another Aboriginal woman (possibly Lizzie) were holding meetings with singing and praise in a tin shed in the centre of Mossman. Eddy Jenkins, who was the first boy to enrol in the newly constructed Mossman Catholic School, used to listen to these women sing (35).

> They were singing in a little sample room next to the Mossman Hotel. The old Mossman hotel. There's a new one there now. Next door there used to be a sample shed where the commercial travellers came to display their wares for the local traders. It was a tin shed.
>
> Sister Hetherington and Sister Rose used to take a religious instruction service there in 1932. Sister Rose was also known as Sister Nellie. She was an Aboriginal woman. There were mostly white kids in the hall. Sister Rose played the piano. She had a beautiful sophrano voice and Sister Martha, an Aboriginal woman played the guitar. She had more or less an alto or contralto voice. Sister Hetherington sang and spoke. I was about 12 at the time. We used to get down to the sample room about 5 or 6 nights a week. She had the service in the sample room when she first came and then they shifted across from the Sergeant's house. The Convent school kids used to give them hell on the way home.

George Edgar Davis supervised the building of the first small cottage at the Gorge out of white-washed flattened tin. Wilma Walker says that "Barney got the boys together to build humpies and they built a house out of flattening kerosene tins for Sister Hetherington. They lived in that tin humpy. They looked after a little boy named Samuel. He died from eating raw corned beef. He's buried up the Gorge." Davis also supervised the building of the first church at the Gorge. Kathleen Bogle (nee Davis) recalls

> we went up the Gorge because Dad was building up there. Mr Johnson from Mango Park let him have as many saplings as he wanted. Dad built a house for Sister Hetherington and Mr Johnson gave him the horses to cart stuff up there. Mr Mullavey donated building materials, nails and a bit of iron.
>
> When Dad got the place going, the people from Daintree came and lived there. They had little huts. There was a big milk tree and we used to get around there with the music going and Sister Hetherington would say "Lord! Send the fire down! Send the fire down!" You'd be amazed that the leaves on the tree were just quivering. The Holy Spirit was outpouring on all those people. They were speaking in tongues and people were saying, "What are they talking about?" It was wonderful.
>
> She had a faith mission. She would pray and things would come in. One day a cheque came from Arnott's biscuits. Big bags of clothes came. I asked her if I could help. She said, "There won't be any money." "It's OK with me," I replied. "There's bags of clothes, you can help yourself."

In a letter to the Director of Native Affairs, dated February 10th, 1948, Ethel Vale describes the circumstances at the Gorge

> In 1930 I accompanied Sister Hetherington together with two accomplished full blood Aboriginals. We came as a mission party on hearing of the need amongst the Aboriginals here, that they had never had a Missionary.
>
> In answer to an inquiry written to the Shire Clerk of Port Douglas, he said not anyone cared for them in that way.

> When arriving in Mossman the Aboriginals were visited and gathered together, also visiting Daintree where they were gathered in and both places were under one heading Our Mission party.
>
> Sister Hetherington toiled very hard and the people followed her.

In the early 1930's, a Church of England missionary, Padre Walkey and family lived about five kilometres upriver from Daintree. Laurie Boswell, (whose family is descended from Dr Johnson's biographer), was born at Port Douglas in 1928. He used to visit the Walkey children as a child and remembers a rented farm house, a thatched roofed building used as a school room and a church.

> I don't think Padre Walkey received any backing from the Church. He had enough money to live on and that was about all. They taught the Aborigines the three 'R's' and also the love of God. Back then, the Daintree Aboriginals were different. They were big men. They didn't drink. They weren't allowed to. They were worth looking at. The residences they built were straight out gunyahs, neat and trim, built out of lawyer cane and palm leaf. Tidy and waterproof too. A lot better than the other huts which were made out of flattened kerosene tins. They were ugly things. There used to be quite a few of them around the place (11).

With Hetherington now living at the Gorge, Ethel Vale stayed in town for another two years, helping "financially and in other ways," before she too, settled on the government Reserve. They were working without any recorded government financial assistance, except for Protector's rations. Smith, Green and Walkey were twenty-five miles further north in the area of the Daintree Reserve. Chant (1997:17) records a visit to Cairns by Hetherington, where she addressed the fledgling Pentecostal congregation.

> A photo taken around 1935, when Maxwell Armstrong was pastor, shows her standing with a group of Cairns people. She was a slight, diminutive, grey-haired woman. She was also said to be hard-working, set in her ways and on fire for God.... Miss Hetherington was a true minister. She was willing to do whatever was needed. One of the rare extant photos of her shows her milking a cow, in another she is conducting a funeral service.

Employers wishing to engage Aboriginal labour were now subject to a Register of Employers, which contained names of those who were considered not fit to employ Aboriginal people. Reasons for this embargo included non-payment of wages and ill-treatment (13).

THE VISION OF ISABELLA HETHERINGTON

In 1935, a suggestion was made to the government to purchase the Almason Estate at Bailey's Creek, just over the Daintree River on the northern side of the Alexandra Range, for the purpose of establishing an Aboriginal Mission by the Seventh Day Adventists who had been administering the Mona Mona Mission on 4000 acres near Kuranda since 1913 (15). Most of the people at Mona Mona were Tjapukai from the Kuranda district and Port Douglas/Mowbray (14) (Wood 1990:5). The Seventh Day Adventist missionaries reportedly saw 80 Aboriginals in two camps at Mossman, 70 in three camps at Daintree and 40 more at Bloomfield (16). Kathleen Myra Bogle remembers

> In 1935,1 completed my time working at the Gorge with Sisters Hetherington and Vale. That was the time that the police were going around picking up children with light skin and sending them to Yarrabah. There was nothing she could do. She wasn't getting any help from the government. She felt sorry for them.

> She said, they had a heart and soul too. There was no alcohol or social security money then.
>
> Sister Hetherington was just like a mother to the Aboriginal people. She'd get a dish of water and wash their feet and tend to them when they were sick. She was a trained nurse and would go to their camps, give them a wash and take care of them. Make soup and feed them. She was an angel in disguise.
>
> She said that she was training as a nurse when she was 15 and had a dream. She said, she saw in the dream all these trees. They were black and distorted and she heard a voice saying to her, "You see these trees?" She said 'Yes, I see them.' "These are the Aboriginal people of Australia, and I want you to go to them." She said, she woke up and she was afraid because she never knew anything about Aboriginal people. She said it stayed in her mind until she finished her training and then she wanted to come to Australia. She got over here alright and then she wanted to meet them.
>
> I met my husband (James Bogle b. Port Douglas of Scottish father and Tibetan mother) in the AOG church, Cairns in 1935. My son, (Ernest) James was born in 1936. When I was expecting another child, Sister Hetherington said, "I want you to give her my name, Isabella," which I did and she was dedicated to follow our Lord and Saviour. And she did right up to her passing to be with Jesus forever.

The suggestion for the establishment of a mission in the Daintree area appears to have come from allegations concerning Japanese beche-de-mer fishermen trading in opium and other goods among the Aboriginals north of the Daintree on isolated stretches of coast (17). The Aboriginal people further north at Lockhardt River had considerable contact with Japanese, Chinese, Islanders, Papuans and Europeans before the Anglican Mission began when the government reserve was transferred there in 1924 (Thompson, 1996:143). There were outrages involving Aboriginal women and unscrupulous lugger captains who were working the beche-de-mer (Thompson, 1996:142/3; Haviland and Hart 1998).

The Chief Protector wrote to the Under Secretary of the Department of Health and Home Affairs who had Ministerial responsibility for Native Affairs

> It is estimated that fully 200 natives, perhaps many more in that district would be benefitted by the establishment of such an institution to control them and protect them from exploitation by aliens (19).

A Ministerial note dated March 1935, decided to take no further action regarding the Almason Estate proposal (20). The Chief Protector again wrote to the Under Secretary in June 1936

> the stage has now been reached when the Department can no longer ignore the pressing need for some action to meet the social and physical needs of the natives of this large district.
>
> There are no less than 230 natives in the camps extending between Mt Molloy and Port Douglas, approximately a further 200 natives in camps between Maytown and Cooktown, without taking into account the number of nomadic and semi-nomadic natives inhabiting the surrounding districts.
>
> There is no established centre between Yarrabah and Mona Mona on the South, and Cape Bedford on the North and none of the three Missions mentioned has resources which would enable them to absorb the large native population in the above-mentioned districts.
>
> In these areas there is practically no suitable employment offering for ablebodied natives or for domestic servants, with the result that practically the entire native population is unemployed and subsisting on native resources with the help of indigent relief.
>
> Quite a number of the natives have funds in the Aboriginal Savings Bank Account which they have earned in past years and

> are drawing on such funds to supplement their meagre resources from hunting native foods.
>
> Indigent relief to an approximate amount of 15 pounds per month is being distributed in these areas, but this assistance is wholly inadequate and does not constitute an effective contribution to the solution of the native problems in the district.
>
> The survey reports of these areas which were furnished by the Director-General of Health and Medical Services, disclose that malnutrition was very much in evidence in these districts and that Yaws, Beriberi and other diseases were not uncommon (21).

Negotiations were resumed with the Australasian Union of Seventh Day Adventists in Sydney and Melbourne (22) and an amount of 2,000 pounds was provided from the Department's Standing Account Estimates (Aboriginal Property Account Funds totalled 14,000 pounds) in April 1937, but here the file ends (23). Presumably, the Almason Estate was considered too expensive. The deed was held by the Public Curator against land tax and rates owing and was not considered for mission purposes.

In 1938, Ps. Charles Enticknap, one of 54 ordained ministers within 39 Assembly of God fellowships (Smith, 1987), built a church on the 'unofficial' mission at the Gorge (25). The Enticknap family lived near Ingham and were foundation members of the Assembly of God movement in Queensland. Agnes Davidson, Charles' sister, was soon to play a major missionary role in the Daintree.

As the decade ended, corruption was found to be widespread within the administrative practice of the Local Protectors of Aborigines (26). In 1939, the 1887 Act and all of its amending Acts were replaced by "The Aboriginal Preservation and Protection Act , 1939" and "The Torres Strait Islanders Act". One of the new provisions required the permission of the

Protector for inter-Aboriginal marriage. The Chief Protector became the Director of Native Affairs. With the advent of the Second World War, large numbers of American and Australian military forces moved into the area. There were Aboriginal servicemen in WW11, but freedom of movement for Aboriginals, unless exempt, was severely curtailed under "the Act".

In July 1940, the Director of Native Affairs received a letter from a Mr Herbert Drake who asked if he could join Sister Hetherington at the Gorge. The Director replied

> although this camp of natives is situated on an Aboriginal reserve, on which Miss Hetherington has been permitted to take up work, she holds no official appointment under this Department, and is carrying on her work in a purely private capacity.

The letter also stated that the number of people living at the reserve included "6 males, 6 females and 8 children(27). However, Drumsara estate, a cane farm adjoining the Gorge, had an Aboriginal camp nearby which was referred to as 'Drumsara Camp'. In the Protector's report for 1940, twenty five men, fourteen women and twenty children were recorded as living there. The Gorge and Drumsara camps were closely situated. Forty men, nineteen women and twenty six children were at the government reserve at Daintree. In August 1940, Pastors Charles Enticknap and Harold Akehurst, currently the Superintendent of the AOG Northern District, called on the Director in Brisbane, where it was agreed that the government reserve at Daintree was unsuitable for a Mission. In his report for 1940, the Protector advised

> native camps are primitive but fairly clean conditions prevail and camps are fairly well looked after. A fair number of natives have been placed in employment as opportunity offers. Native food supplies are fairly abundant and natives not in employment

> subsist on native foods with the aid of indigent rations issued to indigent natives at Daintree. Facilities for education are available at the Gorge and with the Assemblies of God taking up Mission work, Daintree facilities will also be available to impart education to aboriginal children.

Attached to this report was a comment from the Director to the Under Secretary of the Department

> should not some rules covering the control of these Missions or Camps, and responsibilities of maintenance of inmates by the Department and Mission Authorities, be determined?

In September 1940, the Mossman Protector wrote to the Director in relation to the unsuitability of the Daintree reserve which was situated on the Daintree River, a few miles upriver from Daintree township and known to the Kuku-Yalanji as Julayamba. He noted

> the reserve is in reality a fair sized steep mountain, which runs sheer to the banks of the Daintree River. The land is too steep to be cultivated and there is no suitable building sites on the reserve (28).

He went on to advise that with the recent departure of Jardine Green (11), who had been conducting mission work at the Daintree camp, he had inspected the reserve with Pastor Akehurst from the Assembly of God, who had offered to establish a mission nearby. Two days later, Pastor Akehurst sent a handwritten letter to the Director giving his address as 'c/- Mr Arthur Osbourne, "Hillcrest", Daintree via Mossman'

> The present reserve has not enough level land on which to build the gunyahs (being suitable only for camping) let alone do any cultivation. Consequently, the natives have encroached on neighbouring territory and the owner has recently given them orders to vacate. They are looking to us for instructions as to where to go. We are prepared to put a minimum of 100 pounds into a Mission house and school, which may appear rather a

small amount. But we have every reason to believe that more will be available as much interest is being shown by our people in this work. Timber can be procured direct from the saw mill at Daintree, and the labor will be skilled but voluntary.

I am prepared to stay and personally supervise and see to the erection of the buildings and the removal of the natives from their present quarters, and get things in order for approved missionaries to carry on the work. But we must have a suitable reserve to do this.

There is a piece of land most suitable and convenient in every way, 3 and a half miles from Daintree on the Mossman side. -Block No. 115, approx 159 acres. This is available for purchase at a most reasonable figure. Portion has been cleared and been under cultivation. Our aim is to encourage the natives to take an interest in the production of fruits and vegetables both for their own use and for marketing, enabling them to become at least partially self-supporting.

The land is not affected by floods and is convenient both for a doctor's and ambulance attention when necessary. Adjoining this piece of land is a block which is being reserved as a National Park. In the hills is a good supply of water, and, being granted permission, a three-quarter inch pipe could be run from this to No. 115 and an adequate supply of water secured.

If the purchase of this block is considered favourably by your department, it would mean much to us if the matter could be got through expeditiously, so that things could be put on a right footing before the rainy season sets in. Under existing conditions little can be accomplished other than distributing the rations.

We (my wife and self) have appreciated very much the help of the local Protector, Sergeant Rinaldi, who has done all in his power to help us. We realize that the Daintree native is a fine type. We have made as much contact as possible and sought to do all in our power to help them. We have found them most

> responsive. We are anxious to do all in our power to get the work on a right basis (30).

A month later, the Director advised the AOG State Presbytery that there were no funds at the Department's disposal for which a block of land, such as that being suggested, could be purchased. The two thousand pounds offered to the Seventh Day Adventist's three and a half years years earlier was apparently not available. There was some doubt between all parties about the history of cultivation on the block of land which Akehurst had recommended at Kilkeary Point on the Daintree River. Sergeant Rinaldi had ascertained that in Daintree's early days

> this piece of land was worked by Chinese, who grew good vegetables, corn and rice on it, but with the decline of the district the land was thrown up by the Chinese and light scrub has now grown over the places that were previously under cultivation.

Neilsen (1997:62) notes that "a group of Chinese, who had been working the diggings, moved to the Daintree to grow rice. They planted a large area beside the river, but the 1895 flood destroyed their entire crop."

In early December 1940, Akehurst wrote to the Director

> I am endeavouring to arrange a 'treat' for the Daintree Aboriginals. Evidently this has been the custom in times past. Would it be possible for your department to make a small grant towards this? Today, I received per Sergeant Rinaldi the permits re the marriage of Mitchell Roberts to Eva Missionary for which I thank you.

He concluded by advising the Director that he had made a further inspection of the land with experienced farmers who were satisfied with its potential for cultivation and the assurance of water. The Department granted thirty shillings to the Christmas 'treat,' whilst continuing the supply of rations, offering medicine and first aid needs, some school material, and "the usual blanket and clothing issues, similiar to what has been allowed in the past." There were no schools or educational facilities existing for Aboriginal children, apart from Jardine Green who had departed Daintree (Julay) and Sister Hetherington at the Gorge.

It would seem reasonable to assume that the Daintree Kuku-Yalanji appeared responsive to Ps Akehurst's offer of an improved estate. Sexually transmitted disease, morale and despair were major health problems to a people who had seen the "security of their sacred life shattered" (Loos, 1982:43).

Ps. Akehurst met with the owner of portion 115 (approx 145 acres) in Daintree over Christmas and purchased the land. He also purchased the adjoining block, portion 283 (approximately 100 acres) presumably owned by the same vendor. Some of this land was across the public road and unsuitable for agriculture, but most lay along the river. They started building almost straight away. The first building to be erected was a timber church built on a concrete slab by Akehurst, a builder by trade. Two rooms were built at the rear as living quarters. One of these rooms was a kitchen, the other a bedroom. Ps. Akehurst had arranged the purchase of portions 115; and 283, consisting of 259 acres of river flat and forest country lying in a large bend of the crocodile infested Daintree River, at one pound per acre. The land was in the parish of Whyanbeel, 19 miles from Mossman on the Mossman - Daintree Road.

On January 3rd, 1941, Ps. Akehurst wrote to the Director

> All thoroughly enjoyed their outing on Boxing Day. I would like to report that practically all the natives are now located on the property which we have acquired for a Mission Station. The school-hall is now erected almost to completion. We are waiting for the roofing iron which is so difficult to procure under present

> world conditions. The merchant we ordered it from has not been able to obtain his supply and up to the present no stocks are on hand in Cairns.
>
> Our appointed superintendent Pastor H. Davidson, together with his wife and family, is expected to arrive here about January 11th. His fine qualities and organising ability should ensure a good established Mission Station at Daintree.

It was signed by 'Mr H. Akehurst. Secretary for Home Missions. Qld. Assemblies of God.' The Director wrote to the Mossman Protector on 29th January, 1941 asking him to confirm whether "the natives are now settling on the Reserve as contended by Mr. Akehurst." There is a notation referring to lack of roofing iron (it was wartime) that suggests that the Mossman Protector may have intervened, perhaps securing iron from Army stores. Sergeant Rinaldi's reply of 3rd February, 1941 noted

> under the supervision of Rev. Akehurst and his helpers; all the aboriginals who were previously camped on the old Aboriginal Reserve have shifted their camps to the new location. A substantial building has been erected for Church and School purposes and permanent mission workers have taken up their position at the mission.

Ps Akehurst was living nearby in "an old high block house next to Daintree Creek" when Leon Cook and Ted Irish, two AOG church workers, came up on a motor bike to visit the newly opened Mission. Dawn Parker notes "there was no furniture in the house and they all slept on the floor on bare boards. They walked down to a sandy patch on the Daintree River and had the Sunday morning service. People came and joined them from out of the bush" (2).

The Walkey family had now left the Daintree and a new Church of England was built on Dick Fischer's property across the river from the Reserve. Dick Fischer, had just received an exemption from "the Act"(29). Section 33 of the Act made provision for the Minister "to issue any half-caste, who, in his opinion, ought not to be subject to the provisions of this Act, a certificate... that such a half-caste is exempt from the provisions of the Act...". The Department of Family Services, Aboriginal and Torres Strait Islander Records Guide (32) states that

> certificates of exemption were sought by hundreds of people who wished to escape the conditions forced upon them by the Act. In many cases the person wishing to become exempt would write or request the local Protector or anyone else to write on his or her behalf to the Chief Protector requesting to be exempt. The request would often be accompanied by letters of reference which confirmed that the Aboriginal person was of good character and did not associate with other Aborigines.

These characteristics, as well as the ability to manage one's own affairs, were the basis on which exemptions were usually granted. Exemption did not always ensure that a person's money and property would not remain under the control of the Chief Protector. Exemptions could also be revoked at any time (33). The Act was also used by governments to remove Aboriginal people from land where they were considered in conflict with other uses. Dick Fischer is quoted

> Living under the act was a terrible thing. If you left the reserve to get a job and earn some money without permission the police would get you. I received two pounds a week when the average white got ten pounds. They took one pound of that and put it in the bank for when I had no job. I raised my family in their early years on one pound a week, until my youngest child was about six. After I got my exemption papers and my freedom, I was able to earn the same wages as a white person. I was bagging tin and when I came back Lou Fischer told me the Sergeant was looking for me and I thought I was in for a free trip to

> Palm Island. I prepared myself to go there with my family. Palm Island was like a prison. In fact the Sergeant had my exemption papers.
>
> We were allowed into town to do our shopping after we got permission, but we couldn't hang around. We had to walk on the roads - they wouldn't let us on the footpaths. It was good in one way there was no grog. Now they get the Social Services and don't have to work even though there's plenty of work for a strong, healthy fellow. I'd like to see something happen to them. The way they're going on now is no good. I know there's problems now, but in those days it was worse (34).

Dick Fischer, whose exemption was gained by Jardine Green and Lou Fischer, his former employer, paid for his own freehold by scrub-felling at Daintree (29).

The Protector reported that nine children were attending the Daintree mission school. Substantial grass huts had been erected by the Kuku Yalanji on well-drained land, close to the mission hall and nearby the main road from Daintree to Mossman. Meanwhile, Ps Davidson had surveyed 35 to 40 acres for cultivation and was awaiting the end of the Wet season.

ENDNOTES

1. Interview with James Bogle. Mossman, 1997, states that she lived in a house in Grogan St.
2. Letter from Dawn Parker to Ps Westbrook. 8/10/95.
3. Andrew Strachan. Port Douglas & Mossman Gazette 29 /1 / 87. Stan Cummings. Port Douglas & Mossman Gazette. 4 /12/86.
4. Qld Govt Gazette, 16 Oct. 1926, p.1590.
5. 'JAKALBAKU' (Kuku-Yalanji -'book'): 100 years of Douglas Shire Development from an Aboriginal perspective, published by the Douglas Shire Bicentenary Committee in 1988, foreword by

Denis Field. By permission from elders.'

6. 'JAKALBAKU.'
7. Interview with James Bogle, Mossman, 1997, gives his Mother as a witness to such events when she was a "young girl'.
8. William Booth began his evangelistic work in a tent in Whitechapel, London, in 1865. It was then known as the Christian Revival Association. This was changed to the East London Christian Mission in 1870 and extended to cover all London. The title 'Salvation Army' was first used in a leaflet published by Booth in 1878, and it was soon accepted as the name of the whole movement.' Baptised By Fire: The Story of Smith Wigglesworth. 1987. London: Hodder & Stoughton.
9. Sponsored by an interdenominational organisation, the "Christian Covenanters' Confederacy", he preached for two years at the site opposite to where the Glad Tidings Tabernacle now stands. He began with a tent seating 800 and expanded to a canvas cathedral seating 2000. Booth-Clibborn's grandfather, General Booth was with the London City Mission when it gradually became the Salvation Army. He started working with the Church of England and the Methodists (Chant, 1973:110)
10. Hunt was asked to write the story by the then Qld. State Executive of the AOG. His information included 'a number of interviews with old-time Pentecostals and a copy of "The Full Gospel Witness" from late 1929.' Letter to author 9.3.96.
11. The concrete slab of the church where Padre Walkey ministered is all that remains near where the Fischer family live today. A tin and timber church was built by Tom Bruce and Dick Fischer on freehold bought by Dick in 1940. About six people meet on occasional Sundays, on pews taken from one of the original Port Douglas churches.
12. QSA A/58982. This procedure lasted from 1932-1965.
13. Qld State Archive A/58859, letter number 1937/1074.
14. QSA and Dept of Family Services Records Guide. Vol 2.
15. Early Days of the Douglas Shire. Keith & Valda Prince. Published

for the Douglas Shire Centenary 1877 -1977.

16. QSA A/58859. The anthropologist Norman Tindale collected genealogies at Woorabindah, Palm Island and Mona Mona in 1938. Tindale, N. 1974. Aboriginal Tribes of Australia. Canberra: ANU Press.
17. QSA A/58859 extract from Dr. Cilento's report.
18. QSA A/58859
19. Ibid.
20. Ibid.
21. Ibid.
22. Ibid.
23. Aust. Evangel & Glad Tidings Messenger. Vol. 5. No. 8
24. QSA Dept. of Family Services and Aboriginal & Islander Affairs Records Guide. Vol. 1.
25. Queensland State Archives (QSA) A/58838 letter no. 40/1820.
26. QSA R 254 Box 750 6Q/ 2 letter dated 28/9 /1940.
27. Jardine Green obtained an exemption (No. 30) from the 1939 Act for Dick Fischer, enabling him to receive assistance from his former employer, Lou Fischer to purchase the lease on 120 acres at Daintree. Dick paid 100 pounds for the land by scrub-felling. His children live on the land today. Green was known as a missionary and she may also have been a government school teacher.
28. QSA A/58859
29. QSA and Dept. of Family Services and Aboriginal & Islander Affairs, Records Guide. Vol. 1.
30. Ibid.
31. Unsourced press clipping from Lily Fischer (possibly Mossman & Port Douglas Gazette).
32. QSA.6Q/7 10/2/48.
33. Laurie Boswell interview with author. Mossman. 28/11/95.
34. Wilma Walker interview with author. Mossman. 1995.
35. Eddie Jenkins interview with author. Mossman. 19/2/96.

Illustration 5. Nellie and Isabella Hetherington, Mossman 1930s (Mossman AOG collection).

Illustration 6. View of the Daintree River from the mission site 1940 (Mossman AOG collection).

CHAPTER THREE

1940–1943: THE DAINTREE MISSION

The Assemblies of God (Qld) advised the government that the "objects" of the Daintree Aboriginal Mission were

1. To bring to such Australian Aboriginals as may come beneath our care, the Gospel of the love of God unto Salvation through our Lord Jesus Christ.
2. To provide insofar as lies in our power, a place of abode for Aboriginals where they may dwell without fear of molestation; and where they can be sheltered from the vices and evil practices to which they can become subject without such care, and which are not in the best interests of themselves and their children.
3. To provide, to the greatest extent of our ability, for the material well being of the natives by way of food, clothing, medical attention and such other things as may be considered essential to their well-being.
4. To especially care for the children of the Natives that they may start life with good health, and under such conditions as will afford them full opportunities of attaining to manhood and woman-hood.
5. To provide facilities for education for the younger aboriginals.
6. To do, in general, everything that will help the natives in any

way, to live peacefully and happily; and will afford them a sense of well-being (1).

Pastor Hugh and Agnes Davidson and their three children were appointed as the first Missionaries to the Daintree Mission in December 1940. Davidson's father had conducted Pentecostal meetings in the Goulburn Valley, Victoria in 1925 (Smith, 1987:26). Agnes Davidson was born in Halifax in 1907. Her brother, Charles, instrumental in forming the AOG (Queensland) body, was born in Croydon in 1905 where their father, William John Enticknap was a mining engineer at Golden Gate. The family soon moved to Macknade, near Ingham and took up cane farming (2).

The Davidsons left Toowoomba in January 1941 and drove north.

An interview with Agnes Davidson was conducted just prior to her death at the Toowoomba Nursing home in 1995, between the author and the Mossman Assemblies of God Pastor.

Ps Westbrook:	When you arrived at the Mission, where had the people come from?
Agnes Davidson:	All in bits and pieces from along the river. About fifty, sixty, seventy people. They carried their own things, bits of timber.
Ps. Westbrook:	From Barrett Creek too?
Agnes Davidson:	That was all used by the whiteman and cattle.
Ps Westbrook:	What about from up on China Camp?
Agnes Davidson:	I don't know. We never went up there, but there were a few Aborigines living up there.
Ps. Westbrook:	A lot of mining was going on up there.

The area known as China Camp was between Bloomfield and the Daintree. It is reported that Bob Dowell found gold on Gold Hill in the late 1800's. The Dowell range, a short, steep hill divides China Camp from the Daintree. It was a good hunting ground for the Kuku-Yalanji. It was called China Camp because of the many Chinese who prospected for gold and tin in that small pocket about six miles west of Mt Thornton (3). 'Jakalbaku' (1988) gives an Aboriginal perspective of life at China Camp in the 1920s. George Kulka says "'… the Chinese wouldn't have very much to do with us. But the Europeans sometimes enlisted the help of the local aboriginals. Aborigines would swap meat for tea, flour, or rice - sometimes soap, lanterns and kero.'"

In his 1940 report, Sergeant Rinaldi, the Mossman Protector, advised Mr Bleakley, the Director of Native Affairs in Brisbane, that "quite a number of natives through age and physical condition are not fit to work, and would be better off if they were placed on a reserve or removed to a Settlement." In February, 1941, the Director replied "It is mentioned for your information that the Department is averse to the removal of old or indigent aboriginals from their home country to a Mission or Settlement if they are healthy and contented, and their case could be better met by the issue of relief rations."

The Daintree Mission was first established with seventeen huts constructed of grass and old timber with dirt floors. Soon, several rough timber huts were built, some with timber floors and tin roofs. The elderly and sick were allocated a free ration of flour, sugar, rice, tea, meat, potatoes, onions and tobacco, by the Department of Native Affairs and authorised by the Protector. Many of the first residents had been baptised by Hetherington. Agnes Davidson notes

> I don't know how many of them understood the Gospel at first, but it was amazing how many of them prayed. We gathered up every three-penny bit until we got five pounds. The fellow living over the river was growing bananas and pineapples. He let us have some suckers. Hugh planted them and God multiplied them. Hugh had written to the Director of Fruit Culture. He gave Hugh fifty pounds to start fruit at Daintree. That's where it all started.

One of the first tasks was to ask the Douglas Shire Council for an exemption from rates. The Council replied that an exemption could only be allowed on an area not exceeding 50 acres and which was owned by a religious denomination for educational or religious purposes or both. When the AOG State Executive received a Rate Notice for 10 pounds, six shillings and four pence at the end of 1941, the Deputy Director wrote to the Shire Council "this Department recognises the existence of this Mission and it is presumed that after consideration of such position you will not proceed with the levying of rates on the land." The Shire Clerk wrote back reminding the Director that under the Local Authorities Act of 1936, they would claim rates for any area of land greater than 50 acres.

Thompson (1996:151) describes the Mission economy as one which

> required consistent effort, often without immediate gain (or) accumulation of capital and goods for the future. The Aboriginal ethic expected minimum effort with direct results, and when there appeared a benevolent source of supply in the Mission there was natural pressure for it to be snared for immediate needs. Instead, the Aborigines were brought to depend partly on non-natural food sources and on a cash economy. They no longer had full control of the means of production, and became dependent on the capitalist mode of production and Mission patronage.

About 50-80 Aboriginal people were living on the 259 acre Mission, helping to clear the rain forest for a banana plantation, but the number of residents fluctuated. As in times of old, there was much coming and going, with those from Daintree going bush and others from Bloomfield and surrounding settlements coming in to visit relatives. At times, employment was available for the men and their families accompanied them in quarters provided at the place of employment from where they often returned to the mission at weekends. Early morning prayers were held in the church at 7.30AM each day, and every Wednesday the women met under the trees followed by afternoon tea. Thirteen children were being taught by Mrs Davidson at school in the church each day. The Davidson children slept in the church and their beds were rolled up on Sunday. Agnes Davidson continues

> John slept on the floor for twelve months. Pat and Allan had a bunk each in the church which we rolled up each Sunday. We had no nets at first. The mosquitos were terrible. We'd burn a coil every night. We had no tubs. I used to sit in the creek and wash. We had to be careful because the saltwater crocs used to come up.
>
> When we went to Daintree, our wages were two pounds a week for the five of us, but we managed. We were young and we could do it. When you're young, you don't notice hardships. Not hardships. They're fun. A lot of it is fun. You can do it.

When Kuku-Yalanji wanted to withdraw money from their bank accounts to purchase material for the erection of huts on the mission, permission was required from the Protector. Ps Davidson was required to give an undertaking that the huts would remain the property of the Aboriginals. The Director of Native Affairs stipulated that the Mission could not suspend any Aboriginal without permission. Ps Davidson requested and obtained a copy of the Aborigines Preservation and Protection Act 1897, amended 1939, known as 'The Act.'

The average monthly value of rations to the 30 residents thus entitled, was 10 pounds and 7 shillings. The government had not provided any financial assistance towards the operating costs of the Mission. The Protector advised the Director of progress at the Mission.

> It is the usual practise for them to have periods of walkabout for fishing and hunting and they then make the mission their headquarters. Fish are fairly plentiful in the Daintree River and wild pigs and game also abound. No assistance in the food line is at present being provided by the mission authorities, but it is expected with the cultivation of land that a fair amount of produce will be grown for the use of the natives at the mission (4).

Two Aboriginal men, Paddy Henderson and Jimmy Walker, had erected their own huts on the mission. The Director noted that Jimmy Walker "pays maintenance for the upkeep of his son, Norman, at Palm Island Settlement. If he has more children than Norman whom he is supporting, you are requested not to lose sight of the fact that he would be elegible for Child Endowment." Child Endowment payments were introduced by the Lang Labor government in New South Wales in 1927 and nationally by the new Menzies Liberal government in 1941. The Act gave the government the right to deduct maintenance from wages paid into Aboriginal accounts towards the costs of maintaining a Reserve, but Daintree was a Church sponsored Mission. Child Endowment was an entitlement and the government was keen that it should be paid.

After six months, plans were laid to celebrate the opening of the Mission. The AOG publication Australian Evangel and Glad Tidings Messenger (Oct. 1941), reprinted from the Cairns Post (5/8/41), reported

> Pastor Akehurst, N.Q. Superintendent, and Chairman Pastor H. E. Wiggins arrived in Cairns by train and proceeded to the Gorge, Mossman, where nestles Sister Hetherington's Mission for Aboriginals. Sister Hetherington looks frailer than in past days, but is happy to have the youthful vigour and faithful help of our Sister Ena Outen.
>
> A visit to the local Protector (Sergeant Rinaldi) revealed a most sympathetic attitude on the part of the authorities towards our Mission.
>
> We arrived at Daintree at a late hour to be graciously welcomed by the indefatigable wife of the Superintendent, who had been carrying on all the activities of the Mission in the absence of her husband.
>
> Early mists of the following morning presaged a hot day for our tour of inspection of the Mission. It was amusing to see how many natives found excuses at an early hour to cross from the native village to the Mission house in order to catch a glimpse -and perhaps a word - from the visitors. We suspect that many imaginary ailments that augmented the usual morning sick parade had their origin in curiosity.
>
> It was gratifying to note at once that the Mission had settled into a regular routine - sick parade - school for children - rations -village inspection. The religious instruction at the small white school in Daintree township was thoroughly enjoyed. Bro. Davidson gives regular instruction at this school.
>
> Escorted by King Toby, we inspected the native village with its variety of primitive dwellings, some semi-circular in shape, some square, some of grass and a few of iron, but all smoke-begrimed from the inevitable fire so beloved of the natives in the centre of the dwelling. All the natives were proud to be introduced to the visitors, and never failed to pose for the photographer. As we passed on they would break out into the seeming jargon of

their own language and frequent guffaws of laughter followed the visitors, who were left to wonder whether it was at their expense or of the natives.

An afternoon was spent scrambling through the scrub seeing all that was to be seen - the beautiful river - the majestic timber trees - tracks of wild pigs - scrub turkey's nests - the cleared patch planted with paw paw, bananas and pineapples.

That evening the Superintendent, Pastor Davidson conducted a sports gathering for the entertainment of visitors who had already arrived. Spear and boomerang throwing, fire-making and footrunning gave the men folk opportunity to display their abilities; while the women folk gave a display of basket /weaving, flour making and bag plaiting. These proved very interesting to the visitors, who, in the evening, took part in a big campfire meeting.

The mission, which aims at making the natives self-supporting, has been under way for the past six months. In this time, a school has been started, in which the scholars are already showing a marked improvement, the work which was displayed bringing many comments as to its high standard. Along the river bank are eighteen garden plots which speak of the efforts of the natives to better their lot. Pastor Davidson already has a large piece of land under cultivation, and plans are already on foot to convey water by pipeline from the hills to the mission. A very fine avenue of coconut palms has been planted which, in time, will serve as a landmark to those visiting the mission. The little three-roomed houses of the natives look very nice arranged in their rows, while over all seems to lie the appearance of progressiveness which augurs well for the future of the mission.

The visitors included Pastor Wiggins, of Toowoomba; Pastor Akehurst of Mackay; Bro. Dayman, of Townsville; Pastor and Mrs Smith, late of Japan; Pastor and Mrs Irish, of Cairns; and members of the Assembly of God at Deeral, Mossman and Saltwater Creek.

On Sunday July 27, 1941, the Mission was officially opened. The Australian Evangel and Glad Tidings Messenger (Oct.) reported

> Ten thirty a.m. saw a gathering of some 180 persons before the mission church ready for the dedicatory service. The proceedings commenced with the singing of the hymn, 'The Church's One Foundation', after which Pastor Akehurst prayed God's blessing upon the gathering. The superintendent of the mission (Pastor H. Davidson) briefly introduced Pastor Wiggins, who then dedicated the church and the mission to the glory of God and the praise of His name.
>
> The unlocking of the church door was the signal for the congregation to move in and take their places in the church for the service. After the singing of some Gospel choruses Pastor Smith, late of Japan, led the congregation in a prayer of thanksgiving for mercies and benefits.
>
> The mission superintendent then read the Scripture reading, which was taken from Psalm 100 and Psalm 84, after which one of the mission boys, Charlie Sykes, repeated the 23rd Psalm. Pastor Wiggins expressed his appreciation, together with the appreciation of the whole of the Assemblies of God in Australia, to those who had helped and worked and so made the opening day possible. Those to whom the words of appreciation were expressed were as follows: - The Government and Chief Protector of Aborigines for their assistance and counsel; the Sergeant of Police at Mossman, who helped in the finding of the location and many other ways; Pastor and Mrs Akehurst, of Mackay, who laid the foundation of the mission by securing the property and building the mission church; Mr and Mrs Osbourne, of Hillcrest, Daintree, for their assistance and material help; Miss Hetherington, of the Gorge, Mossman, and King Toby, who was so keen and helpful in shifting the people on to the mission, finally, Pastor and Mrs Davidson, late of Toowoomba, who had left all at the call of the Lord and came to North Queensland to superintend the mission.

> Following some items of song by the Daintree people, Pastor Akehurst, Northern district Superintendent, spoke on the words of Psalm 92: 1, "It is good to give thanks to God." The next speaker was Miss Hetherington who spoke of the early days of pioneering among the natives in the North. At this juncture, Pastor Irish sang the negro spiritual, 'Come, Come to Jesus'. Pastor Wiggins then spoke from 2 Chronicles 46: 41 - 42, the theme of which was the erection of Solomon's temple and Solomon's prayer for the continual presence and blessing of God.
>
> The service closed with the singing of the hymn, 'Onward, Christian Soldiers'.

In September 1941, the Mission applied to the government for financial assistance. It was recognised that the mission was on private land and not a government reserve. The Protector had suggested that Mrs Davidson receive "a small allowance" because a permanent salaried teacher was not justified. He also considered they be afforded some assistance to clear the land for cultivation.

The Australian Evangel and Glad Tidings Messenger (Sept 1941) reported that "parcels of clothing (were) most gratefully received, especially in the line of men's clothing" were provided by southern Assemblies. North Queensland was viewed as a 'Home Missions' field by the Assembly of God, who urged their Assemblies to support this work. There were twenty AOG church fellowships in Queensland by 1941. In November, the Mission claimed child endowment for three children in their care, furnishing a statement of costs incurred in establishing the Mission and an estimate of the first twelve months of operation, totalling 834 pounds, 16 shillings and three pence. (This included the cost of the land at 180 pounds, the church building at 176 pounds, nine months salary for Ps. Davidson at

123 pounds and a missionary's residence under construction at 260 pounds.)

A considerable area of land had been planted with fruit and vegetables and Davidson requested administration of Aboriginal matters in the Daintree district. The Department was experiencing difficulties in the area of child endowment payments. Some recipients desired cash whilst others could not make a signature. Aboriginals had to sign with the Protector when starting employment and when operating their bank account. The nearest banking facilities were at Daintree as well as a store, butcher and baker. Davidson pointed out that Mossman, being the headquarters of the Protector, was 22 miles distant and at certain times of the year "contact was well nigh impossible." He added that if the Department favoured his application, as was the case at Mona Mona and Yarrabah Missions, he would be able to attend to the needs of people on the spot. It would relieve the Protector of the necessity of proceeding to the Daintree when matters arose.

In early 1942, the Davidson's moved into a house opposite the church, comprising a kitchen, dining room, two bedrooms and an office. Their former living quarters at the rear of the Church, became a store from where staple supplies, such as bread, flour, sugar, rice, potatoes, onions, cheese, condensed milk etc. were available at cost price. April came and went and Davidson had received no reply to his request for administration of Aboriginal Affairs at Daintree. Meanwhile, the threat of World War Two was given as reason to remove residents of the Cape Bedford Mission near Cooktown and their long-serving German-born missionary, 74 year old George Schwartz was imprisoned. The 254 Aboriginals boarded ship at Cooktown and cleared the Endeavour River for Cairns. It was their last view until well after the war. Some went to Yarrabah, but the majority were railed hundreds of miles south to Rockhampton and from there to nearby Woorabindah Mission Reserve. Many did not return. In 1943, the hospital ship 'Centaur' was hit by a Japanese torpedo off the coast of Queensland, with the loss of 268 lives.

The Daintree Mission continued to plant bananas and pineapples; while the Department of Health conducted a 'Hookworm Campaign.' In October, the Director advised Ps Davidson regarding his application for District Administrator that the Solicitor-General had ruled "this land being Freehold cannot be declared an Aboriginal Reserve. It will first have to be surrendered and then reserved under the Lands Act." As they celebrated Christmas 1942, there was a change of Protector at the Mossman Police.

ENDNOTES

1. Letter, dated 28th November 1949 to the Director of Native Affairs, Brisbane.
2. William (Snr) and Charles were foundation members of the Qld AOG when it formed in 1929.
3. Claude Leroy personal conversation.
4. Letter from Mossman Protector to Director 17/9/41. QSA -A/58859.

Illustration 7. Isabella Hetherington milking 'Trixie' a "dear old quiet cow" and a gift to the mission by "folks whom we befriended in time of sickness" (Pat Davidson collection), Daintree Mission, January 1942.

Illustration 8. Early huts at Daintree Mission, 1941 (Mossman AOG collection).

Illustration 9. The Davidson family, with neighbours on left. AOG Chairman and N.Q. Superintendant Ps H.E. Wiggins on right, leaving Toowoomba December 27th 1940 (Pat Davidson collection).

Illustration 10. The opening of Daintree Mission in 1941 (Government archives).

CHAPTER FOUR

1943 –1945: THE NEW PROTECTOR

Although it could have been decided by correspondence, the State Chairman of the AOG, Ps Henry Wiggins had elected to take the matter of surrendering the Daintree Mission from freehold to government reserve before a meeting of the full State Executive. The situation at the Gorge reserve is described by the Department of Native Affairs Inspector Richards who wrote to the Director on 7/9/43.

> While in North Queensland recently an inspection was made of the Gorge Mission in company with Sergeant Moran, Protector of Aboriginals at Mossman and Mr. G. Roberts of this Department. This Mission is under the control of Sister Hetherington, an elderly lady 73 years of age, who has one assistant also advanced in years.
>
> Sister Hetherington is in receipt of the Old Age Pension and her administration of the Mission is hampered by lack of funds. Nevertheless the condition of the inmates is satisfactory and no fault, apart from sanitation, can be found with her management of the place. The permanent residents on the Mission number six (6), but this number is greatly increased over holidays and week-ends and at times eighty aboriginals are in residence for short periods.
>
> There are no sanitary conveniences of any description and in accordance with your instruction, the matter was discussed with Mr Kelly, Government Health Officer at Cairns, who

> stated that five cesspits were necessary. Mr Kelly expected to visit Mossman about the end of last month and promised to try and secure this number of conveniences in that centre where a number of people are installing septic systems and will have no use for their existing W.Cs.
>
> This Reserve is favourably situated about two miles from the Township of Mossman and comprises an area of approximately 64 acres of good quality soil capable of growing fruit and vegetables for the use of aboriginals. There is an excellent water supply, the water main supplying Mossman, having been tapped near the intake.
>
> This Aboriginal Reserve would be ideal for use to accommodate all the coloured people in the Mossman-Daintree areas at a later date if required.

After twenty seven years the government reserve had "no sanitary conveniences of any description" save that occupied by the Missionaries. Cesspits built some years earlier had collapsed and soil pollution existed. The administration of the 'Mission' was hampered by lack of funds and toilets were to be obtained from the backyards of Mossman residents when they converted to the septic system, even though the town water supply flowed through the reserve.

The government policy of protection and preservation did not extend to sanitation. This is the first mention that the government might move all Aborigines in the Mossman-Daintree area to the Gorge Reserve. At Daintree Mission, Davidson restated his desire to be delegated the position of Mission Superintendant. The Director reassured him that his office "actuated a desire" to assist him in his work but was bound by the Solicitor-General's ruling. Meanwhile, the new Protector claimed that he had received complaints from employers regarding the supply of Aboriginal labour from Daintree Mission. Employers alleged that Pastor Davidson kept the Aboriginals working on the mission, rather than releasing them for employment. In May 1943, the Protector complained

> this man interferes too much with the aboriginals in employment, which only means extra work for me as Protector.
>
> The boys about the mission gamble every Saturday and Pastor Davidson has not enough control over them to stop it. I have been confidentially informed that a signed petition is on the go about this District regarding Pastor Davidson's interfering with the employer and employee. I am told that the Daintree Mission is supposed to be self-supporting, but I cannot see anything at the Mission that would be self-supporting apart from a few banana trees and pineapples. This man has been continually asking me to have all the aboriginals sent to Daintree Mission under his control, but I can assure you Sir, if this is done and he is given full control over the natives the Police will be doing nothing else but patrolling to Daintree.

The policy that allowed for children of 'mixed descent' to be removed was in force at the time: 'A child with a non-Aboriginal biological father was as a matter of official policy to be removed from its mother and placed in an institution' (1). Kathleen Bogle, interviewed in 1996, said that Sister Hetherington who had been "very sick a couple of times," didn't like the removal of children and that there weren't many "light skinned" children at the Gorge. Wilma Walker was living there.

Wilma: Government come and they do this to me. "That little girl come here!" I'm the only one was there. All the half-caste ones they grabbed him and sent him away. They used to hide them in the basket. Big basket.

RG: Where did they send those half-caste children?

Wilma: Oh. Yarrabah. Everywhere.

RG: Why'd they do that?

Wilma: I don't know. Police just went crazy. Grabbed them and sent them away. Old people see police come, "Hide! Hide!" They grabbed me and put me in the basket. They put me right in the corner. All the old people everywhere, the police couldn't see through. Before I got married the old people said, "Come here!" They all talk, sing out and sit around and sing. They put me in the middle. They got the fire sticks and run them around me so nobody could get me. Catch me. Police or anybody.

Sister Hetherington was looking for little girl to teach, so we could go to school. Sister Hetherington and Nellie and this one lady came along, Sister Vale and they came to my friend Eileen MacNamara. They was teaching. This lady got me, take me to town, make a room for me and teach me how to cook, sweep up, set the table and all that. Eileen, my sister, both of us was working there. But I was always thinking about the Gorge. I wanted to go back and teach them.

They sent Norman Walker away to Palm Island. Them old people say, "See this boy here? When he come back, you're gonna get married to that boy."

Many of the Aboriginal men were now cutting cane around Mossman. There was no accommodation for their wives in the cutter's barracks and wine and other drink was easy to obtain. An Inspector found the situation where the Mission in trying to protect Aboriginals from exploitation, was guilty of attempting to control their movements in relation to outside employment whilst the Kuku-Yalanji living under the Act were numbered according to a government file. When the file did not square with a person, e.g., 'S - 62' seeking rations, the Protector alleged that Ps Davidson had changed their names and confused the identity cards. Ps Davidson vented his frustration in a letter to the Director on October 5th, 1943

> we are in this job to help the aboriginals, spiritually, morally and physically; and not for any benefits to ourselves; and we have received plenty of bumps for our efforts, though we are spending ourselves freely; my wife especially wearing herself out slaving for our aboriginals.

WEDDING BELLS

The marriage of Paddy and Nellie Mossman was the first wedding at Daintree Mission. Agnes Davidson recalls that Nellie "had been a Christian for some time. She pleaded with the Lord. Lord Jesus! Make my heart clean. She used to look nice. We used to make white calico dresses for her and we found some white sandals. I kept them for her. She used to wear a white apron. Everything was white." Isobellala Hetherington was a guest at the Daintree Mission on occasion. "We did everything we could for her,' said Agnes. "She said to me 'I'm going to give you every bit of my poetry. A box of it. I'm giving it all to you.' I regret that she didn't give it to me. She was quite good at it. The government might have it somewhere."

In November 1943, Aboriginal labour from outside the mission, possibly men from Palm Island, were chosen by the government to make improvements, constructing conveniences. On the 17th December, Davidson wrote to the Director

> I am enclosing Mr Maxwell's invoice for the timber and iron which we secured from him for the building of the conveniences. The invoice is not itemised but I can get Mr Maxwell to prepare

> one if necessary. Re the two boys Charlie — and Wilkie — who came up to do the work. We put them up in a room at the back of the Church and they were going to batch but my wife offered to feed them; and they jumped at it and we said they could pay 12/6 each for a week and they were more than satisfied. They were here one week and had no money when they left and promised to send it out but they have failed to do so. The amount they owe is 25/-. We aren't so particular about the money, but I know that Charlie — at least, squandered what he had and could well afford to pay his way. Charlie took the responsibility of meeting the amount for both.
>
> As far as we can ascertain most of the natives are using the convenience and we hope they all will ere long.

The European custom of providing a building for toilet purposes was different to that of most Aboriginals who were not familiar with sanitary closets. This was the first time that many had lived in a European style settlement.

WATER ON TAP

The end of financial year report at June 30th, 1944, lists some of the Mission improvements under Davidson's administration

> A water supply was the most urgent need and we were most fortunate in being able to secure sufficient new galvanised piping to bring excellent water by gravitation from a creek in the hills. Previously the natives had to carry their water about one third of a mile from the creek and the supply was not sure or very clean during the dry season. We put in 2 inch pipes and should have sufficient water to irrigate quite an area of garden as well as supplying the needs of the village. (Lot. 116 on which the spring was located was 160 acres and leased from the Crown at 1 pound per annum.) Items taken from the Mission Account Books for your interest:

COPY. FA. 19/9/44.

18.7.44

DAINTREE MISSION.

Trading Account for year ending 30th June, 1944.

To Purchases	78. 5. 9	By Sales	69.16. 6
" Provision for Labourers	28. 0. 0	" Consignment Sales	392. 2. 0
" Wages of Aboriginals	94.12. 6		
" Freight (Inward)	6. 6. 2		
" Profit & Loss	254.14. 1		
	£461.18. 6		£461.18. 6

Profit & Loss A/c for year ending 30th June, 1944.

To Stamps, Phone etc.	1.19. 3	By Trading Account	£254.14. 1
" Consignment Freight	28. 7. 0	" Donations	132. 8. 0
" Commission	40.18. 3		
" Transportation	17. 8. 5		
" Depreciation	1. 4. 6		
" Food for Indigents	30. 0. 0		
" Mission Account	267. 4. 8		
	£387. 2. 1		£387. 2. 1

Balance Sheet at 30th June, 1944.

ASSETS.		LIABILITIES.	
Petty Cash	5. 0. 0	Mission A/c (Capital A/c)	308. 6.11
Water Scheme	265. 4.11	H. Davidson (Portion of this is money held in trust by me for others). (Itd). H.S.G.	75. 0. 0
Chevrolet Truck	70. 0. 0		
Buildings	9. 9. 6		
Fencing	12.13. 7		
Plant	11. 5. 7		
Furnishings	1.17. 1		
Cash in hand £5. 9. 7) Cash at Bank 2. 6. 8)	7.16. 3		
	£383. 6.11		£383. 6.11

DAINTREE MISSION.

It is to be understood that the figures on the back hereof as regards Assets are incomplete, they only represent the increase in Assets as recorded in the Daintree Mission Account Books, and even in this they are incomplete as no charge has been made for Wages in the ~~in the~~ installation of permanent Assets as the Water Scheme, buildings etc. The whole of the wages paid out are shown as a charge against Profit and Loss. In future wages incurred in permanent improvements will be added to that improvement.

(Sgd). H.S.G. DAVIDSON.

72

Illustration 11. Daintree Mission financial account 1944.

> Income — Gross sales of Mission Produce — 461 pounds, 18 shillings and sixpence. Donations received — 132 pounds and eight shillings.
>
> Expenditure — Water scheme — 265 pounds, 4 shillings and eleven pence. Motor truck — 70 pounds. Fencing — 12 pounds, thirteen shillings and seven pence. Plant -11 pounds, five shillings and seven pence. Wages paid to Aboriginals - 94 pounds, twelve shillings and sixpence. Food for Aboriginal labourers — 28 pounds. Food given to needy Aboriginals - 30 pounds.

In September 1944, the Director returned a copy of the accounts with a note of thanks. They were tabled at the Biennial Conference of the Queensland AOG in Townsville the same month. After travelling to Brisbane for a meeting with the Director, the matter of having the mission declared a government reserve remained unresolved. The government's estimate of the property was below the three thousand and twenty five pounds asked by the AOG. Ps Davidson was concerned by the lack of resolution and agreed to make a recommendation to the general presbytery as soon as possible. It was his wish that the mission be gazetted a government reserve rather than stay as a freehold property (3).

In 1945, the 'Aboriginals Regulations' was added to the provisions of the 1939 Act, continuing the policies outlined in the 1897 Act and increasing the powers of the Director of Native Affairs in relation to Aboriginal property, courts, police and gaols. The increase in control was extended to superintendents on government reserves and an Aborigines Welfare Fund was established by the Treasurer The fund was made up of monies derived from sources including proceeds from the sale of reserve produce and store sales, deceased estates, fines or fees, and interest from all trust accounts.

Jimmy Walker, who had erected his own hut at the founding of the Mission had been paying maintenance for his son Norman on Palm Island and asked that he be brought back to Daintree.

Agnes Davidson: My husband got Norman out of Palm Island. His mother was taken to Palm Island. I think she was taken because she had that white baby, half-caste baby. Now, isn't that cruel. He was brought up on Palm Island. Norman told my husband how he got belted by the cane every day, no matter if he was good or bad. He said, we were encouraged to do all the wicked things we could do because we'd get the cane whatever we did.

He told my husband he'd work for him for nothing, rather than go elsewhere to work. "You sharpen the tools," he said. "They don't sharpen them over there." He had been working somewhere. But Hugh wouldn't let him work for nothing.

The Protector's allegations that the Daintree Mission had failed in providing Aboriginals for outside employment, reached a climax in April, 1945. The Aboriginals declined to work for certain white men and were interviewed by the Protector. They sought the support of Ps Davidson, but the Protector interpreted this as interference in their manner of employment.

I might state here that Johnny O'Gilvie (J 129) of late has become cheeky towards white people and it is imperative that he be given employment immediately for his own benefit. Is Mr Davidson allowed to have natives working on the mission property without agreement? If this is so it means that there is

> no check at this office as to any monies paid to the aboriginals and it is undermining the Aboriginal Protection Act as these are openly stating that they do not intend to work under agreement. The profits derived from the sale of fruit from the Daintree Mission on which these boys work runs into hundreds of pounds and I have no record of any aboriginal receiving any of the profits derived from the sale of this fruit.

The Director wrote to Davidson "you are now requested to advise why you used influence against these men entering employment at a time when labour is urgently needed." This, and other relevant correspondence was copied to the Mossman Protector. Again, Davidson refuted the allegations. He advised that he would be in Brisbane during the next month and would give the reasons why he did not support O'Gilvie and Bamboo's employment agreement. At that meeting, accompanied by the Superintendent of the Northern District of the AOG, the Director was advised that the AOG Conference had refused to agree to the handing over of the Mission to the government for reservation purposes. Ps. Davidson stated that he intended resigning from his position at Daintree because of the decision. Meanwhile, the Mossman Protector was taking statements from the offended employers and the Aboriginals.

In August, 1945, Ps Davidson advised the Director that he objected to Bamboo being signed on to a particular man

> (or anyone in Mossman) for I am sure Bamboo does not wish to be signed on to him, and I know it would not be in the best interests for him and his wife and family to go into Mossman.
>
> They are happy and contented here, and cared for, and Bamboo can secure work in the Daintree area. Bamboo's wife Katie returned here from Cape Tribulation at Christmas time last year and she and the children were in a dreadful state and it is only just recently that she and the youngest boy have recovered...

> If the Protector at Mossman had the interests of the Natives really at heart, he would not try as he has to get the natives with their wives and children into Mossman, where they pick up plenty of sores and where cheap wine can be readily purchased by the natives at extortionate prices. The Mission is now in a financial position to fully support the children with the help of Child Endowment; and I wish to apply that the Mission be registered as an Institution for Child Endowment purposes and the Endowment paid direct as was suggested previously, but the Mission was then unable to make up the balance.
>
> I would be grateful if you would send the necessary forms for completion and return to you. In this connection it will be best also for us to be reasonably sure that the children wouldn't be moved away from here, except at your express wish. To sum up, it's a tough job to try and superintend an aboriginal mission under an unsympathetic Protector.

Cape Tribulation, named by Cook in 1770, from where Katie Bamboo returned, was known to the Kuku-Yalanji as Kurranji meaning 'cassowary' (Neilsen, 1997:59). Davidson, who had declared himself opposed to the forced removal of children, was advised that as it was not' a government reserve, it was not possible for it to be registered as an Institution for the receipt of Child Endowment monies'. The only person entitled to sign for child endowment was the mother of the children. An offer was made by the Director to allow mothers to collect their entitlement at the Mission store by making a 'book-up'. That same day, the Director sent a letter to the Commissioner of Police.

> It is desired to record the unsatisfactory manner in which the Protector of Aboriginals, Mossman, carries out his duties as Protector and your co-operation in an insistence on the reasonable prompt attention to aboriginal matters generally would be appreciated.

A letter requesting an investigation into the plaintiffs' fitness to employ Aboriginal labour was also sent. On both cases, the letters referred to the Protector's ability to report on complaints made against Davidson. On the 29th October, 1945, the Sub-Inspector's Office at the Cairns Police Station investigated. The subsequent report upheld the complaints against Ps. Davidson

> The good feeling which is desirous and very necessary in the control and management of the Aboriginals at Daintree Mission, does not exist. This state of affairs is undoubtedly responsible for the delay by the Protector in attending to matters relating to Aboriginals attached to the Daintree Mission. I understand that Pastor Davidson and his wife are to leave Daintree Mission in the very near future, which should bring about more happy relations between the Pastor at Daintree Mission and the Protector.

The investigation concluded that there appeared to be dual control of the Aboriginals in part of the Mossman Police Division by the Protector and by the Pastor of the Daintree Mission. On the 23rd November, 1945, the Director wrote to Ps. Davidson requiring him take note that unless he made Aboriginal labour available to the plaintiffs "an Officer from this Department would visit your centre and definitely allocate labour not being utilised on the Mission, to work where it can be profitably engaged for the good of the country".

The situation that Ps Davidson found himself in was not without precedent. In 1887, the Missionary Carl Meyer arrived at Cooktown Reserve from Bethesda Mission in South Australia. Timber-getters were already on the Reserve and at first sought permission from Meyer to cut the timber. Evans (1969: 57) notes

> the Government, more concerned over the disreputable character of the timber-getters and their detrimental affect on the Aborigines, refused to grant any timber licenses for the

> Reserve area. Dr Roth (the Protector) was intensely antagonistic to the presence of the timber-getters on the Mission and described them as a "lot of black-guards". The residents backed by the Chamber of Commerce continually asked the Government to reserve its decision as regards the cancellation and discontinuance of timber parties. They "point(ed) out that the timber will never be any use to the Aborigines". The mission had curtailed the supply of cheap labour to the residents, a policy which incited considerable animosity towards Meyer.

The taking of timber from government reserves was seen as having no value to, nor impact on the lives of Aboriginal people. Encroachment on Aboriginal reserves for timber-getting was a feature of European behaviour. Agnes Davidson remembers the situation that brought them into disrepute with the Protector and employers who considered they had a right to Aboriginal labour

> It was a big offence if you tried to stop an Aborigine from going to a job. This boy, George Bamboo, was a big strapping fellow. He was a good worker. They all liked him. He met this fellow way up on Barrett Creek who arranged for him to get on the bus to Mossman. They went every Monday and Wednesday. We put our mail bag on because the children were on correspondence school.
>
> This man told George to come in on Monday and he'd be on the bus too. George went in but the fellow wasn't on the bus. Another fellow in Mossman saw George and said, "Come and I'll sign you on."
>
> "I can't," he said. "This other man's coming in." This fellow talked and talked and got him to go and sign on. He went up to the Police Station and he signed on and then came home to get his things. The other chappie came along on the next bus and went for him. He took him back to the Police Station and made them rub it all out and he signed George .on.

This policeman, I've forgotten his name, used to come home drunk. His wife would ask the constable to help her put him in the lock-up where he'd sleep it off. The natives said that was a fact.

One day without any notice, a car pulled up in front of our place and out jumped three officials from the Department of Native Affairs in Brisbane. They wanted to see me, not my husband. They asked me about George Bamboo. I told them it was ridiculous what the Sergeant must have written them. He wouldn't have known without coming up to see what it was all about. They said to me, "I believe the Aboriginal people give you some money and you buy their things when you go to Mossman?" We went in once a month. I said, "That's right." And he said, "Have you got that written down in the book?" I said, "Yes." "I'd like to see it." he said.

Off I ran and got it. Hazel Easton happened to be visiting us, or living with us for a while. I said, "Make three cups of tea. Give the nicest cups you can get and the nicest tray cloth and could you get a teapot enough for three men with the nicest biscuits you can find."

"Yes," she said, "I'll do that for you."

She got the tea ready while he looked through the book, turned its pages all over and looked at it and handed it back to me. Never said a word. I should have taken Hugh's books out. He was a perfect bookkeeper (4). I said to these fellows, "I'll show you the plantation now." We walked through grass up to our eyes, you know what it's like, right down the road, down to the bottom where the river turned. That area was always acres of bananas. There wasn't a weed in the place. It was per-r-r-fect! Everything was cultivated.

Hugh would run the prongs over the soil when it was soft after rain and everything was beautiful. When we walked out past this high grass, they stood there and gasped. They got the shock of their lives. All these bananas all bagged. The big tall

GM Gross Michael bananas were at the back - tall trees - and then the Cavendish and the pineapples in front. The pineapples looked pretty. Some of them had real red leaves. We couldn't use the others. If you had a shower of rain, they'd fill up with water and ferment.

We did all our own packing. All our bananas and pineapples went up to the American camp on the Tablelands. We had brand new boxes and nice white paper. We found that if you present the best, you get a much better price.

On the 30th November, 1945, Pastor Davidson notified the Director that he was resigning his position at Daintree to take up Pastoral duties at Rockhampton.

I am handing over the superintendancy of this Mission on 3rd December 1945, to Pastor J. Easton, formerly of Brisbane. Ps.Easton has been here for some weeks now settling in to the routine of the Mission.

Yours of the 23rd instant arrived yesterday and I will delay the answer to some points till I see you but I feel duty bound to state that the facts re (the complainants) are as I have stated, and that the report you received was not based on a thorough investigation. Further, it would be doing aboriginals a grave injustice to force or persuade them to sign on to him and I, personally, would not in any way encourage aboriginals to do so.

I also repudiate the suggestion that co-operation between me and prospective employers is not what it should be. During the five years of our time here I have done my utmost to persuade and encourage the aboriginals to accept work offering in this district.

As I told you previously I will not tolerate able-bodied men hanging about the mission doing nothing. I would suggest if you send an Officer from your Department he would not find much labour to allocate at the Mission but he would find some lounging around Mossman, supposedly unemployable, also up the river from here there are some aboriginals and a number of

> Lockhardt River aboriginals. At least they have been there for some weeks and most of them still are as far as I know.
>
> Apparently my word counts for very little but I would remind you that I have disinterestedly put in almost five years in a genuine attempt to help these natives and I can truthfully say that quite a deal has been accomplished that has been beneficial to them. A few weeks investigation by an incognito unbiassed private detective would give a pretty fair picture of things as they are.

The Davidsons were unable to meet with the Director; Mr O'Leary due to his absence from Brisbane. However, he later acknowledged that the crate of pineapples which they had sent to him were an excellent sample.

ENDNOTES:

1. Queensland State Archives & Department of Family Services and Aboriginal and Islander Affairs, Records Guide. Vol. 2.
2. Fred Johnson. DJAWAL IDI. Ab. Educ. Resources Unit. East Perth. 1985
3. He wrote to this effect on the 15th November, 1944.
4. Ps Davidson held a Diploma in Book-keeping and Business Methods from Stotts College.

Illustration 12. Unidentified man at Daintree Mission 1940s (Mossman AOG collection).

Illustration 13. Anna - "extracting milk from green ants." Daintree Mission 1941 (Mossman AOG Collection).

Illustration 14. "Villagers", Daintree Mission 1940s (Mossman AOG collection).

Illustration 15. 'Sister Hetherington's faith mission to Aborigines, Mossman, 'Nth Qld Funeral Service.' Isabella Hetherington conducting funeral at Mossman Gorge Reserve, circa 1930/40. (Mossman AOG collection).

CHAPTER FIVE

1946 – 1949: THE DORMITORY

In December 1945 Ps. Jack and Hazel Easton took over the daily affairs of the Mission. Jack had recently been discharged from the Army and arrived at Daintree Mission weighing ten and a half stone.

> In January, I took sick with a fever. The doctor came out once a week and was treating me for Mossman fever. I'd be alright one day and the next, I'd have a raging temperature, vomiting, and the next day up and about, then down the next with a higher fever than the previous day.
>
> I was getting worse and worse. They got the ambulance out and took me to Mossman hospital. That was on a Thursday. On the Saturday, a relative of Hazel's, George Conwell, who was in the Army in Cairns came out on the White Car Bus at midday. He saw what condition I was in and he caught Jimmy's bus at one o'clock back to Daintree. He told Hazel, "You'd better see Jack. He won't last much longer." We had no phone so she just changed and got the five o'clock 'picture bus' into Mossman.
>
> There was no bus home until after the pictures around midnight. We never had cars in those days. On Monday, they decided to send a blood sample to Cairns. The result was positive malaria. So they gave me some quinine. I was down to 8 stone 13 Ib and they kept me in for an extra week. I was on crutches and didn't have the strength to walk, but I had to put on some condition to get back to the Mission.

> When I got back, Norman couldn't start the truck, so I had to get out of bed and fix it. Not that I was a mechanic. Oh, no. I wasn't a mechanic. That was the early days of the fruit. I took over the Daintree Mission growing bananas and pineapples after four years in the Army. I wasn't a farmer. We had to fall the scrub by cross-cut saw and axe, do the logging and burn the scrub off. It was hard yakka. We used to dynamite the roots of the trees out of the ground and level it off. We had the rotary hoe. I taught Charlie Sykes and Norman Walker how to use it and then we'd dig the soil over and plant the suckers and the pineapple tops and the butts. We had to spray, bag them and keep the flying foxes off.

To assist the Eastons, an assistant was provided by the AOG. Daphne Dales was among the first. Norman Walker had returned from Palm Island the previous year. Wilma Walker describes those times at the Daintree Mission when the Eastons took over.

> I was working in Mossman. Used to bank my money, working, working. Them old people came from Daintree, check up on me all the time. Norman was looking around for me. Old people said, "Your girlfriend's coming now!" The men and boys were digging that road through the Mission, down to the mail box where the banana shed was. "Oh!" they'd say. "Your girlfriend getting bigger now!" Norman was working on that farm. He know he's gonna get married to me, build a house. He was banking too.
>
> They asked policeman for Norman to get married. "Send Wilma to Palm Island?" Norman say, "No! I keep him at Daintree. Look after him with clothes and everything." I told my boss, "I'm leaving." He says, "Alright." He got another girl. I go to Daintree and got a job looking after all the Bama (Aboriginal) kids with Sister Easton. When I went up to Daintree Mission, I didn't know nothing. Didn't see another boy, just going along. My Grandma, my sister, those ladies got me then.

> Sister Easton said, "I'll teach you how to sew." I made a wedding shirt and a wedding dress. We built a house. My husband build it on the ground first and all the men lifted it up. Then we got married by Pastor Easton and live in that house. I got married young and skinny at 16. He was 20.
>
> **RG:** The government records show that your husband applied for permission to marry you on the eighth of January, 1941.
>
> **Wilma:** Yeah. Happy time.

THE PASSING OF ISABELLA HETHERINGTON

On August 31st 1946, Isabella Hetherington passed away in Mossman hospital at the age of 75 years. Ethel Vale was with her when she died. Ps. Easton was in Brisbane on Mission business and a Brisbane Presbyterian minister, who was a Methodist minister in the north, the Rev. Robert Missenden conducted her funeral.

> She was a beautiful woman with snowy white hair down to her waist. I was supposed to pray for her, but she prayed for me. I was with her when she died. I had read about what happened in books, but this happened before my eyes. She sat up in bed and said, 'Lord Jesus. I am coming.' Then she lay back and was gone (Hunt, 1978).

Isabella Hetherington was buried in an unmarked grave in Mossman cemetery the following day. Her death certificate was witnessed by Herbert Drake, who had in 1940 sought permission from the Director to join her at the Gorge. Drake's wife had died some years before and he had come north with two young sons. The Shire Council suggested that they put a tap in Mossman in memory of Hetherington but "some wanted it and some didn't" (1). Chant (1998:7) notes Hetherington "declared that the Mayor of Mossman, who had assisted the

DEATH

DEATH in the District of Cairns in the State of Queensland.

1946 Registered by Edwin Lancelot Moore District Registrar

Marginal notes (if any)	Column		
	1 Number	4683	14338
	DESCRIPTION -		
	2 When died and where	31 August 1946 District Hospital Mossman	
	3 Name and surname; profession, trade, or occupation	Isabella HETHERINGTON Missionary	
	4 Sex and age	Female 75 years	
	5 1. Cause of death	1. Hypostatic pneumonia 2. Acute gastritis 3. Hookworm infestation	
	2. Duration of last illness	1. days 2. days 3. years	
	3. Medical attendant by whom certified	Dr G. Corones	
	4. When he last saw deceased ..	3 August 1946	
	6 Name and surname of father .. .. Profession, trade, or occupation ..	William Hetherington Property Holder	
	Name and maiden surname of mother	Rebecca White	
	7 Signature, description, and residence of informant	Certified in writing by A.M. Garson, Matron District Hospital, Mossman	
	8 1. Signature of Registrar	E.L. Moore	
	2. Date	3 October 1946	
	3. Place of registration	Cairns	
	If Burial or Cremation Registered - 9 When and where buried or cremated	1 September 1946 Mossman Cemetery	
	By whom certified	A.E. Crimmins	
	10 Name and religion of minister, and/or names of two witnesses of burial or cremation	Robert T. Missenden Methodist Hopp Drake T. Kirkpatrick	
	11 Where born and how long in Australian States, stating which	Ireland 44 years	
	If deceased was married - 12 1. Where	-	
	2. At what age	-	
	3. To whom	-	
	13 Issue living, in order of birth, their names and ages	Living	years
	Deceased, number and sex	Deceased	

CAUTION:- Whosoever shall unlawfully alter any Certified Copy of an entry in any Register of Births, Marriages, or Deaths, whether by erasure, obliteration, removal, addition, or otherwise is guilty of a CRIME, and is liable to the punishment by law provided in that behalf. (Vide Sections 486 and 488 of the "Criminal Code.")

I, Alistair Douglas Dodds , Acting Registrar-General, do hereby certify that the above is a true copy of an entry in a Register of Deaths kept in the General Registry Office at Brisbane, and I further certify that I am a person duly authorised by law to issue such certificate.

Extracted on 18 April 1996

Acting Registrar-General

N.B. Not Valid Unless Bearing the Authorised Seal and Signature of the Registrar-General

Illustration 16. Isabella Hetherington's death certificate.

work of the Mission in many ways, would not die before he turned to the Lord. Years later, after her death, this came to pass."

On the day of her funeral, Ps Easton was at a government meeting in Brisbane accompanied by Ps Davidson, now the Secretary of AOG Home Missions and another AOG representative, where it was made plain that the government could not appoint a Superintendent unless the Daintree Mission was made a Reserve The following month, the Mossman Protector advised the Director of the death of 'Miss Isabella Hetherington,' adding

> since the return from Brisbane of Pastor Easton, I have several enquiries from natives of the Gorge Mission, and also others who reside at the Gorge mission, re their being sent to Daintree Mission. It appears that on Easton's return, he has contacted the aboriginals and informed them that they are all to be sent to the Daintree Mission, and that the Government is taking over same and that he will be in charge. This has caused a lot of discontent amongst the natives at Mossman, and it will mean them going anywhere and every where if they have to go to the Daintree Mission, they do not want to leave Mossman, and if they do the boys now under agreement about Mossman, will also go as their wives will be at Daintree, and instead of being under agreement they will be hanging about the Daintree Mission.
>
> In view of this matter I would like to know the position, as the natives are coming to the station every day inquiring about same, and my own personal opinion of the matter, is that they should be left at the Gorge mission, Miss Vale is capable of carrying on at the Gorge Mission (2).

Ethel Vale was well-respected, small in stature and reportedly had no need of a microphone when she sang. Laurie Boswell describes her voice as being "like thunder. Fantastic.

They loved her, although mostly she was timid and retiring" (3) (4).

> Sister Vale lived up there without anyone with her after Sister Hetherington died. Daphne Dales came to help her for quite a while, but she wasn't very happy because conditions were not very nice. Meg Robinson came up and took charge. Meg Robinson was a Scottish woman. A very big woman. Daphne and her got on extremely well together.

The water had been assayed as "100 per cent pure" at the Gorge and a quantity of grapes, lemons, mandarines, paw paw, bananas, custard apples, sweet potato, pumpkin and other vegetables were under cultivation (5).

Jack Easton returned from Brisbane.

> I went up with the truck to Daintree each Friday morning to get the rations and do Religious Instruction at Daintree School (6).

> I used to leave Norman Walker in charge of the boys to cut the bananas, gather the pineapples and put them at the end of the road. We had a butcher at Daintree and any shopping was done at Osbourne's store. I'd come back and unload. Hazel and Daphne Dales issued the rations to the natives while I drove down and loaded the bunches of bananas onto the truck. Then I'd bring them up to the shed, unload them and go back for the pineapples. On Monday, Tuesday and Wednesday, we got timber from the sawmill at Mossman or Cairns. Jimmy Martin would deliver and we'd make cases. On Friday afternoon, we'd dehand all the bunches of bananas and stack them up to let the sap drain off. Saturday morning, we started packing the bananas in cases. We'd be packing all day till midnight because we wouldn't work on the Sunday.

> We'd have church and then visitation in the afternoon, service in the evening. Then at two in the morning packing, ready for Jimmy Martin at six o'clock. We built a litttle shed down at the mouth of the road into the Mission. We'd load the produce into

> Jimmy's truck and he'd take them right through to Mossman. That was the program in the peak season. The hours we had to work. Sometimes you used to get half a penny a pound. That was hard yakka. We used to sell some of the suckers and butts, thousands of them. That was a good income with the farmers around Daintree and we used to get gifts from the different Assemblies.

The Aboriginal workers were paid according to the provisions laid down by the Department of Native Affairs. The number of workers employed in the cultivation and packing of bananas and pineapples varied according to the seasons. They were provided with all meals on working days and rations on weekends.

In September 1947, a statement was sent to the Director of Native Affairs listing the gross income from sales of fruit and produce for the past three years in pounds Sterling:

1944/45-1348 pounds.

1945/46-1098 pounds.

1946/47-1217 pounds.

In those three years, a total of 1275 pounds was paid in salary to Aboriginal labour. In October 1947, the General Secretary of the AOG in Queensland, Edward Irish, wrote to the Director offering the surrender of the Daintree Mission Property for 3000 pounds, provided the AOG could carry on the 'religious side of the work'. The registered proprietors were William Harold Akehurst, William John Enticknap and Hugh Stanley Giffard Davidson as trustees. The two portions comprising 258 acres and a further 160 acres (Allot. 116 leased from the Crown for water) were in the County Solander, Parish of Whyanbeel. It was freehold with no encumbrances. Included were livestock, a Chevrolet truck, plant, building materials, stock in store, fencing, a water scheme, missionary's house, furnishings including a refrigerator and an organ, church building, sheds, Aboriginal bathroom and washhouse, four acres of bananas, two acres each of pineapples, citrus, pasture and cleared land. The Department of Health and Home Affairs felt that the price was much higher than the value, and after an inspection in November 1947, they declined the offer. The AOG then offered the Mission under a Deed of Trust,

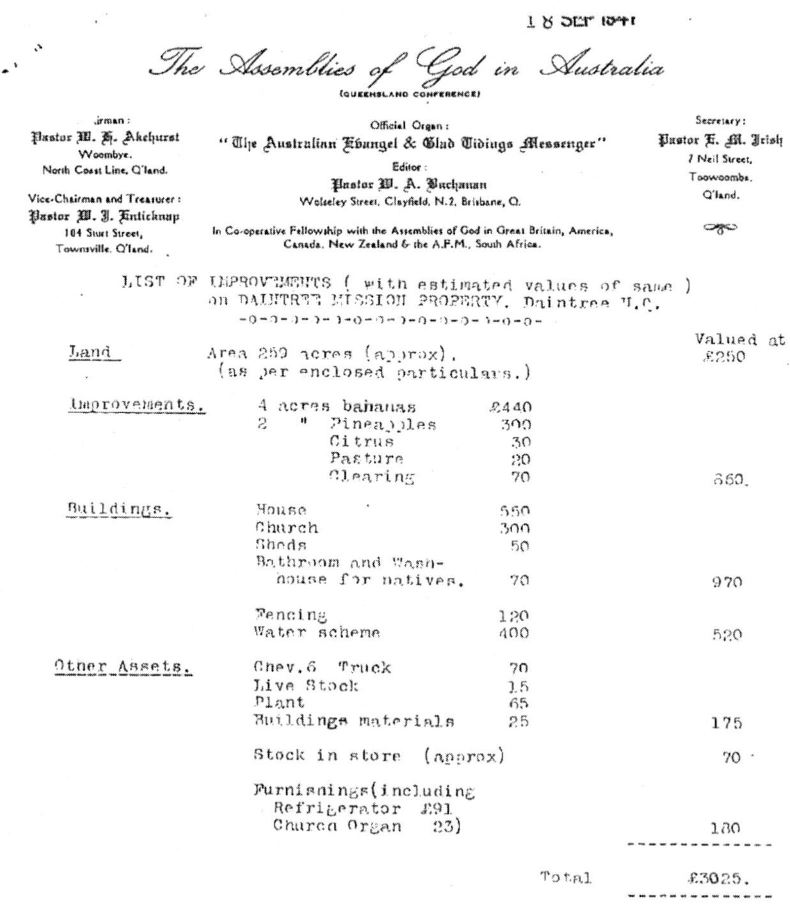

18 OCT 1947

The Assemblies of God in Australia

(QUEENSLAND CONFERENCE)

Chairman:
Pastor W. H. Akehurst
Woombye.
North Coast Line, Q'land.

Vice-Chairman and Treasurer:
Pastor W. J. Enticknap
104 Sturt Street,
Townsville, Q'land.

Official Organ:
"The Australian Evangel & Glad Tidings Messenger"
Editor:
Pastor W. A. Buchanan
Wolseley Street, Clayfield, N.2, Brisbane, Q.

In Co-operative Fellowship with the Assemblies of God in Great Britain, America, Canada, New Zealand & the A.F.M., South Africa.

Secretary:
Pastor E. M. Irish
7 Neil Street,
Toowoomba,
Q'land.

LIST OF IMPROVEMENTS (with estimated values of same)
on DAINTREE MISSION PROPERTY, Daintree N.Q.
-0-0-0-0-0-0-0-0-0-0-0-0-0-0-

			Valued at
Land	Area 250 acres (approx). (as per enclosed particulars.)		£250
Improvements.	4 acres bananas	£440	
	2 " Pineapples	300	
	Citrus	30	
	Pasture	20	
	Clearing	70	860.
Buildings.	House	550	
	Church	300	
	Sheds	50	
	Bathroom and Wash-house for natives.	70	970
	Fencing	120	
	Water scheme	400	520
Other Assets.	Chev.6 Truck	70	
	Live Stock	15	
	Plant	65	
	Buildings materials	25	175
	Stock in store (approx)		70
	Furnishings(including Refrigerator £91 Church Organ 23)		180
		Total	£3025.

Illustration 17. Improvements to the Daintree Mission in 1947.

providing that in the event of the property ceasing to be used as an Aboriginal Mission, it would revert to the AOG.

During the 1947/48 Wet, a time of monsoonal rain and cyclone between December and April, the Mission was isolated and they had to rely on food in the store for six weeks. When the flood had subsided, Easton and fellow workers walked down to Barrett's Creek, took the little punt across and walked five miles to Daintree for supplies. Bananas and pineapples were taken down to Brother Douglas at the church in Cairns and occasionally, the Mission children went to nearby Miallo where Ps and Mrs Easton held meetings.

At the Gorge, after nearly twenty years of service Ethel Vale was thinking about a long holiday. On February 10th, 1948, she wrote to the Director of Native Affairs

> Dear Sir,
>
> Please excuse the liberty I take to write to you.
>
> The local Protector of Aboriginals Sergeant Mr Neaven called yesterday with a letter, he received from you, which he gave me to read.
>
> In which I note your mention of the bad state of lavoratories. I might mention that a few months ago, the health inspector together with the hookworm campaigner Mr Thompson were here, and I understood from Mr Kelly, health Inspector they would send someone to attend to them.
>
> We had not sufficient help at the time or it would have been attended to long ago. Am sorry.
>
> And now there is some helpers, and they are being attended to right away, both the mens and ladies lavoratories being fitted up with newly made cabinets, also disinfectant. There are also a number of improvements in progress, such as cleaning up, planting food stuffs etc.

> Sister Hetherington who has been a marvellous pioneer Missionary for 44 years and who laid down her life for these remnant left... passed away two years this August. She prayed that some help would come if the natives were still to be ministered to as it is an ideal place, plenty of good water... Sister Hetherington beautified the grounds in a marvellous way.
>
> So I have been in charge since Sister passed away. I have anticipated a change away after, going on 18 years to see my aged Mother being now 89 years, also two Brothers who are ill.
>
> After praying about the situation, one day I was visited by a Mr Kramer whom we had known many years ago about 80 years, he has been in mission work among the Aboriginals. His wife who is now deceased was a school teacher who had the school, and Mr Kramer did the other part as a Missionary at Rolands Plains N.S. Wales. He had wanted for years past to get here especially while Sister Hetherington was here. In company with him is a man and his wife by name Mr & Mrs Ross. So all three have offered to stay till I return and they are real labourers....
>
> The holiday will take three months at least.
>
> So pending your approval or disapproval
>
> I remain
>
> Yours obediently
>
> (Miss) Ethel M. Vale

Vale refers to the same Ernest Kramer, who as a young Swiss immigrant married to Effie Buchanan had met Hetherington in Melbourne in 1912. The Kramer's, with a young son, journeyed to South Australia and from there, began a covered wagon ministry among the Aboriginal people to the north and central Australia (7). A contemporary of Reverend John Flynn, the Presbyterian minister later known as 'Flynn of the Inland', Kramer, at eighty years of age had come to Mossman and Ethel Vale took leave of the unofficial Mossman Gorge Mission.

In the centre of Mossman, at a place known as the Junction, there was an Aboriginal camp known as Junction Camp where approximately 13 Aboriginal people were in permanent residence. A new Protector had been appointed and he wrote to the Director on 10th March,1948

> I understand that this is an unauthorised camp situated on the property owned by Mr. W. H. Mullavey at the end of Junction Road. Mr Mullavey agrees that the camp should be moved. There is no sanitation, the natives camped there make use of the nearby bush for sanitary conveniences, and this is very unhealthy. There are six sub-standard shacks built at this camp in which the natives live. I am strongly of the opinion that the natives should be moved to the Gorge Aboriginal Reserve,
>
> Mossman, and the sub-standard shacks demolished. The State Health Inspector is also of this opinion.
>
> I am informed that there is another camp known as Bridge Camp off the Daintree Road, Mossman on the bank of the Mossman River, which also has no sanitary conveniences and the bush nearby is used for that purpose. I am of the opinion that this camp should also be demolished and the natives moved to the Gorge Aboriginal Reserve, Mossman. I am informed that the land where the camp is situated is owned by Mrs. A. A. Raldini. It is an un-authorised camp and the owner would not object to its removal.
>
> I have been informed by the State Health Inspector that previously the Junction Camp was demolished by Native Tradesmen who were sent here to do the work, and who also put in the cesspit conveniences at the Gorge Aboriginal Reserve, Mossman.
>
> Perhaps arrangements could be made at your office for Tradesmen to be again sent to Mossman to carry out the work necessary to establish proper Cesspit conveniences at the Gorge Aboriginal Reserve, Mossman.

Shortly after, cesspits were begun and new vegetable gardens planted. There was a change of personnel at Native Affairs in Brisbane and a new Director replied to the offer of surrendering Daintree Mission under a Deed of Trust. On the 18th June 1948, he informed the Under Secretary via an internal memo

> The establishment of a Church Mission in this area is not considered desirable. It is accordingly recommended that the Church Body be informed that the Queensland Government does not propose to establish any further Church Missions for aboriginals at present and that their offer cannot be accepted.

THE DORMITORY

Hookworm was a major health problem affecting Aboriginal children. In some cases they were taken into protective care by Ps Easton at Daintree Mission.

> Nellie and Paddy Mossman had a girl who they called Agnes. They also had little Lenny. Nellie wasn't a robust woman. She took sick, so my wife Hazel and I took Lenny in. Then we got Nellie in, so we had to put a verandah on the back of the house.
>
> We put blankets and that on the floor and they slept there. They were used to it in their own place. We had children coming up on the Mission. Some of them survived all the problems and troubles. There was Lenny Mossman, who was about four. His mother had died. Agnes who was Lenny's sister and Clare and Doris Gibson, so we decided we'd go ahead and build a dormitory.

There are differing points of view about the controversial function of mission dormitories. Green (1996:168, 208) writes "the practice of semi-nomadic people leaving children at mission schools was regarded by Elkin as normal behaviour for those trying to adapt to a new economy. The missions willingness to take care of children left parents free to pursue tribal affairs while intending to recover their children as it suited them." Meston (1896:9) noted that Deebing Creek mission "is also a home for the children of those blacks who like to leave them in safe keeping while they go away for an occasional ramble."

In relation to the Forest River Mission, W.A. in 1914, Green (1996:197, 208) notes that

> when the children's dormitory was completed and surrounded by wire netting topped with two strands of barbed wire, the camp Aborigines were fed outside the compound. The rule served two purposes: it reduced the likelihood of elders luring children from the school and it limited cultural transmission from the older generation to the young converts. Although the white population of Wyndham, less than 100 kilometres as the crow flies, represented a threat to the moral welfare of the young, it would appear that the real threat to (missionary) Gribble's teaching was the influence of the traditional Aboriginal culture... yet it seems that in most cases recruits were willing volunteers.

An Aboriginal woman who lived in the Yarrabah Mission dormitory, notes "Dad Gribble was very strict, but we were very fond of him... They were really lovely days, those days, even though we had the discipline" (Higgins, 1981:15). A. P. Elkin, an anthropologist and Anglican clergyman, compiled a negative report on the administration of Ernest Gribble at Forrest River in 1928 (8). In 1930, a girl's dormitory was established at Lockhardt River Mission north of Daintree and described as a building "without bolts and locks and without problems of girls running away" (Thompson, 1996:147). In 1938, the dormitory was closed, but reopened "when it was felt that the girls were not being adequately looked after" (Thompson, 1996:147).

Rowse (1993:27) notes that Rowley referred to the term "inmates" to describe residents of missions and reserves and that institutionalisation was central to the Aboriginal experience of colonialism. Jeremy Long, one of Rowley's research assistants, estimated that "one third of the 75,000 Aboriginal people enumerated in 1961 lived on government or mission settlements - seventy-eight establishments in all throughout Australia" (Rowse, 1993:27). Like many other aspects of Christian Missions, the dormitory experience was relative to the mission, its time in contact history, and the personality of missionaries and protectors. Harris (1990) writes

> to shield Aboriginal girls from, unscrupulous and immoral whites was not pettiness; it was life-saving. To rail against immorality was not narrow-mindedness, but a commendable concern to stem a great social evil. It was not wowserism, but courage. In these sanctuaries, Aboriginal young people survived. They married and produced healthy children. Many became Christians. Their descendants are alive today. The missions became places of hope for the future.

After witnessing Hetherington's death certificate, Herbert Drake, who was still living in Mossman with his two sons, rode a bicycle to the Daintree Mission each day to help build the dormitory behind the church. It was a weatherboard building erected on high concrete blocks. The lower section was enclosed with glass windows and a concrete floor. There was a well-equipped kitchen where the eldest girls helped prepare meals for the labourers. In addition, there were dining, schooling, bathing and laundry faculties. Upstairs had a roomy front verandah and an airy and pleasant dormitory with the Matron's room adjoining.

Daphne Watkins who arrived at Daintree in late January 1949, was the first matron when the dormitory opened in late April that year. There was a six foot paling and wire fence around the dormitory which was breached a couple of times. Its purpose was to protect the girls from sexual predators but

Watkins prayed and it was taken down (9). Facilities were later added to accommodate young boys. Daphne Watkins was dormitory matron at Daintree Mission until October 1952.

> During the time (three and a half years) that I was there, six more girls and one boy (total of fifteen to date) came to live in the Dormitory, and three left - one to be married, one went to Cairns to work and the third was taken by her mother. With regard to this little girl, she was two months old and her mother was unable to care for her, so the Police Sergeant, who was the Protector of Aboriginals for the area, ordered that she be put in the Dormitory until she was two years old. As soon as she turned two her mother took her away.
>
> The aim of the Dormitory was to provide the girls with a new and better way of life and teach them how to care for a home, and also to improve their education. Up to that time the children were taught the three "R's" by the Missionary ladies, but their attendance at school, not being compulsory, was very irregular. With the advent of the Dormitory the children were given regular school lessons, first with Correspondence School lessons and then at the nearby State School. The older girls helped with the washing, cleaning and cooking.
>
> Their spiritual education was not neglected, we had regular devotions and they were encouraged to read their Bibles and pray. There were also times for regular exercise and play. During Easter 1952 Daphne Dales, who was stationed at the Gorge Mission, and I brought 12 girls and two boys from Daintree to Brisbane by train for six days. We attended a Youth Rally at Glad Tidings Tabernacle and took the children to see some of the sights of Brisbane, including the Lone Pine Koala Sanctuary and the City Hall tower (10).

Ps Easton advised the Deputy Director that Wilma Toby, Mary Anderson, Hilda Spider, Marjorie Denman, Doris Gibson, Kathleen Winkle and Agnes Mossman, ages ranging from four to eighteen living in the dormitory at their parents request. The latter two had been in the care of Mrs Easton since March, 1948. Easton wrote 'the girls are being educated in every possible way; the older girls being taught general household duties and care of themselves, while the younger girls - Kathleen Winkle and Agnes Mossman -are enrolled with the Primary Correspondence School, Brisbane are making good progress with their lessons." Alice Marbach, who was dormitory matron from January 1959 to April 1962, notes

> in our dormitory at Daintree, at least during my time there, no child was forcibly taken into the dormitory The children were there at the request of their parents, except for one child who was dying of asthma. I asked for her and in a few months of drier housing and better nutrition and by God's grace, she became a healthy child free of asthma (11).

In 1949, the Aborigines Welfare Fund required the Protector to deduct from the wages of all persons employed under the Act, contributions to the fund at the rate of 5 per cent of gross earnings for people without dependants and 2.5 per cent for people with dependants. If the employee was a resident of a settlement or mission, but employed outside the settlement or mission, a deduction of 5 - 10 per cent of gross earnings was made for settlement maintenance, but the Daintree Mission was not a government settlement. The Mission accounts show that wages were paid to Aboriginal workers who paid for their own houses, without having to subsidise Mission costs. Medical attention was provided by Mission staff and a weekly visit from the Doctor at Mossman, whilst infant care was provided by mission staff or a Bama (Kuku-Yalanji) mid-wife.

The Protector sent a letter to the Assistant Deputy Director on 23rd May, 1949, informing him that a young Aboriginal woman whose parents were deceased

> was becoming troublesome in the Mossman area and finally she was persuaded to live at Daintree Mission. Under the supervision of the Authorities there, her conduct has greatly improved, the girl is now being taught to read and write and generally looked after by keeping her apart from the young men.

In 1949, Dot Stennett was at the Gorge Reserve Mission assisting Ethel Vale who had returned from leave. On the 27th April, 1949 Stennett wrote to the Mossman Protector

> On the 20th April, 1949, I commenced a daily school on the Gorge Mission for the benefit of the aboriginal children of Mossman. It is my intention to teach the children, for a few hours each day, five days a week, as long as I am at the Mission and there are children to be taught.
>
> At present I have five (5) children enrolled but I'm hoping to have others who, at present, are living in various parts of Mossman. Your cooperation in this matter will be greatly appreciated.
>
> The slates and reading books I have are wearing out, borrowed and insufficient for the number of pupils. Would it be possible for you to secure for me the necessary school materials through the Director of Native Affairs, please?
>
> Some medical supplies would also be very useful for the natives on the Gorge Mission. Attached hereto are suggested lists of useful necessary goods.
>
> Yours truly,
>
> (Miss) D. H. Stennett
>
> Supt. Gorge Mission.

The history of some pioneering Aboriginal missions in north Queensland reveals, although there were exceptions as Missions were dependent on the personality of the missionary and situation, (Anderson 1984:327; Guy 1999:19), that missionaries began formal schooling in English and, in some documented instances, indigenous languages "long before any

State educational authority considered it worth their while to do so" (Berndt 1988a:47-54). The Northern District Protector, Dr Roth (1899:8) notes that in the 1880s, the Cape Bedford Mission school was conducted in the local language of 'Guugu-Yimidhirr', with the assistance of an Aboriginal Christian (a Diyari man from Bethesda Mission) and Johannes Pingalina, as well as in English. However, after 1900, the Preservation and Protection policy became entrenched along with the 'Doomed Race' theory, (McGregor 1997) eugenics and biological assimilation, until Assimilation policy began in the late 1930s (Evans 1969:14-34; Hasluck 1988:67-68; Marine 1998:57-59; Read 1998:18; ATSIC 1998:10).

The Mossman Protector, Sergeant McNeven recommended that the articles Stennett requested be supplied, "as it will be to the advantage of the aboriginals concerned". He wrote on 28th April, 1949

> I have to advise that an inspection of the Gorge Aboriginal Reserve, Mossman, which is occupied by Indigent and other Natives, disclosed that undergrowth and grass is out of control and growing right up to the camps, which will be a great fire risk when the dry season sets in, quite apart from the untidy appearance of the surroundings.
>
> Inquiries disclosed that the natives have no tools with which to keep the place clean, and I have been requested by Male Indigent Relief Recipients to obtain tools for them to clear the undergrowth, and also to make a garden in which to grow green vegetables.
>
> Under the circumstances I would recommend that the following tools be forwarded for use by the Indigent Natives at the Gorge Aboriginal Reserve of which Miss Vale is in charge.
>
> 2 Brush-hooks with handles, 2 Reaping Hooks, 2 Rakes with handles (Iron Rakes), 2 Chipping Hoes with handles, 1 Garden

Spade, 1 Garden Fork with handle, 1 Maddock with handle, 1 Hammer with handle, 2 Flat files.

Ethel Vale was supervising child endowment for, but at the Daintree Mission, as some of the children were technically being cared for by the Eastons in the dormitory, the Department decided that their mothers were not entitled to further child endowment payments. The Department advised the Mission that they should register as an Institution under the Child Endowment Act. The Mission's books were audited in preparation.

In late 1949, ten girls were living in the Daintreee dormitory when Leila Gallienne, a student at the Commonwealth Bible College at New Farm in Brisbane, heard that there was an opportunity to relieve Daphne Watkins.

> We had finished our Bible School for the first year and I said, "Well, I'll go." So I went home and packed my bags, hopped on the train and came up to Cairns. I slept in Sister Watkins room in the dormitory for two months. It was a very nice time. King Toby's daughter was in the dormitory. Not Wilma. A younger one. Seventeen years old.

Ps. Easton: There was only Frank and Wilma Toby. Brother and sister. They were the only children of King Toby.

Leila Gallienne: This was supposed to be his daughter. Might be his grand daughter. The only boy I remember in the village was Charlie Denman. (12) He was fourteen. A fine fellow. But he didn't want to go to school, so he hid 'round the back of the house while you drove them to Daintree school in the Mission truck. Clare Ogilvie was an albino. She was a lovely little girl. They went to school everyday. The boys in the village had to go too.

I organised the children to cook. There were no babies in the dormitory. The youngest was about three or four. We had meat and rice. When I came up, I was nice and heavy and when I went back, I was three stone lighter. I wasn't starving. I just didn't eat much. I organised the washing. You had to tell the girls what to do. Sometimes they would sneak out and have a little rest. Those girls were aged up to sixteen. I was twenty-three.

One day we decided we'd like to climb a big mountain over the road. The bigger girls - we left the little girls at home with someone -and up we went. It was beautiful. A lovely place. We went this way and we went that way and we got lost. It came time that we should go home. And I said, "Where are we?" King Toby's daughter came to the rescue. She said, "Let's follow the creek down?" So we did, found the road and went home. We were lost in the bush. An awful feeling it was.

Ps. Westbrook: Where were these kids parents?

Ps. Easton: They were on the Mission.

Ps. Westbrook: So you just gave them accommodation and fed them.

Ps. Easton: The parents visited them. They still had a relationship with the parents. When we started the dormitory, the parents were willing to give us the children. It was at their request that we decided to build the dormitory. They didn't have to pay to come into the dormitory. They never gave us any money. I've forgotten how we got the money, but we got it. We had good women to care for the children and they were happy there. Katie Bamboo, a relative saved Clare O'Gilvie from her mother, Elsie O'Gilvie. Her mother got a fright when she had an albino baby. She was going to kill it.

Laurie Boswell: Johnny O'Gilvie was going to kill Elsie.

Ps. Easton: Before we finished the dormitory, we took her on our verandah and we cared for her with the request of the parents, Elsie and Johnny Ogilvie. They gave her to us and we looked after her. The newspapers have said she was taken from her parents. They said she was placed in a dormitory against her will. She was always happy there. The newspaper was incorrect (13).

Clare O'Gilvie was born at Daintree Mission on the 23rd December, 1944 (14). Her father, Johnny O'Gilvie came from China Camp and her mother, Elsie was born at Cooktown. The O'Gilvie's gained exemption from The Act in 1962.

RG: How did your parents come to be living in Daintree Mission?

Clare: Dad was a drover. He was droving cattle through many places, travelling everywhere. They made a home at Daintree Mission and Mum stopped there. Mrs (Wilma) Walker was mum's mid-wife for me. Mrs Walker was not married yet. Ps Easton put me in the dormitory and I went to school at Daintree School.

When I first went in the dormitory, none of the girls wanted to talk to me. They didn't want to play with me. They didn't want to have nothing to do with me because I was a white one there. They said, "We don't want to play with little white one like you!"

RG: How did that make you feel?

Clare: I couldn't understand myself. The matron had to explain it to the girls. There was one girl there who looked after me very well. Cathy Winkle. I used to be with her most of the time. She used to get me into a lot of strife (laughs).

RG: Has it always been hard for you knowing that you're an Aboriginal, but people thinking that you're a whitefeller?

Clare: People been asking me questions. Tourists said to me, "You're skin is very fair. You're almost like a white person. We always see you with the Aboriginal people." I told them I'm an Aboriginal 'cause my mother and father are Aboriginal and I've got really dark brothers and sisters. Mum was frightened. Dad was working and Mum didn't know what to do when she think that Dad is going to kill her because he think that she been playing up with a white man. She couldn't understand it either.

I had to recognise myself as an Aboriginal and tell people my story about what happened years ago at Daintree Mission. About my parents. I've got a brother, Paul. He's the same like me.

RG: What do you think makes a person aboriginal?

Clare: When George and Katie Bamboo took me, they sort of adopted me. There was some tourists always coming up to Mrs Bamboo and wanting to give money for them to adopt me, to take me away, but they said, "No. If she go away she won't be able to come back and know, identify her people."

RG: Did you like growing up on the Mission?

Clare: Yes. The rules were very hard and strict, but you had to go by the rules. Matron Biddle, she was very hard. Her and Cathy couldn't get on.

RG: Did you go to church there?

Clare: Yeah. We learnt about Jesus. They taught us how to say Grace at the table.

RG: Do you think that is still good for your life?

Clare: I really thank God for saving my life. I believe in my heart that God was right there at the time of the incident when my Mum and Dad was get rid of me. I pray for my own people.

ENDNOTES

1. Agnes Davidson. Personal interview. Toowoomba. Qld. October. 1995.
2. Ps. Jack Easton says he knew nothing of such a move. "The Protector would have to process the paperwork before such a thing could happen, the Mission being freehold." Letter to author dated 6/3/96.
3. Leila Gallienne, relieving dormitory matron, 1949, adds "she was a lovely old lady. She went down to Brisbane because her body was worn out."
4. Laurie Boswell agrees with this description of Sister Vale, but says that he finds it difficult to agree with the description of her voice. "She always struck me as a very nervous little lady, very quiet. There could be a 'tangle' between her and Meg Robertson."
5. Letter to director of Native Affairs from Ethel Vale. QSA 6Q / 7. 10 / 2 / 48.
6. The State Education Acts Amendment Act of 1910 legislated that instruction should be given "in the primary schools during school hours in selected Bible lessons from a separate reading book to be printed for the purpose." A departmental committee was appointed to compile Readers in accordance with the Act and a series was produced which was still in use in the 1940's.
7. E. Kramer, Caravan Mission to Bush People and Aboriginals, Journeyings in the Far North and Centre of Australia, n.d.

8. For further information on Rev. Gribble's career, see The Reverend Ernest Gribble by Christine Halse. Lectures in North Qld History. Townsville: JCU. 1996: 245. James Noble of Yarrabah by Geoff Higgins. 1981.
9. Dawn Parker letter to Ps Westbrook. 8/10/95.
10. Daphne Watkins letter to author. 10/8/96.
11. Alice Marbach letter to author 23/7/9618.
12. Charlie passed on in Cairns Base Hospital, July, 1996.
13. Brisbane Courier Mail (11/12/93).
14. O'Gilvie interview with author. Mossman. December. 1995.

Illustration 18. Isabella Hetherington and friends, Mossman 1940s (Pat Davidson collection).

Illustration 19. Monday Shuan and family with Davidson children, Daintree Mission 1944 (Pat Davidson collection).

Illustration 20. Ps Jack Easton, Daintree Mission 1945 (Mossman AOG collection).

Illustration 21. Pineapple and banana plantation, Daintree Mission 1940s (Mossman AOG collection).

Illustration 22. L to R. Norman Walker, Paddy Mossman, Hazel Easton, Lenny Mossman, Jack Easton with Daintree Mission bananas 1946 (Mossman AOG collection).

Illustration 23. Harry Shuan, Daintree Mission 1948 (Mossman AOG collection).

Illustration 24. The opening of the dormitory, Daintree Mission 1948 (Mossman AOG collection).

Illustration 25. Dormitory children, Daintree Mission (Mossman AOG collection).

CHAPTER SIX

1949: SORCERY AND CULTURE

In 1960, Norman Baird, a Kuku-Yalanji man informed anthropologists that sorcery was "still practised and belief in it is still very strong" (H.& R. Herschberger 1964; Jakalbuku 1988; Erbacher 1991:62, Thompson 1982:17). Reser and Eastwell (1981:310) write that sorcery functions in Aboriginal society as a means of control, "other avenues of customary Aboriginal social control are foreclosed because they involved physical attack and injury which now offends white Australian law." The presence of missionaries ended "summary killing" for 'payback' practices on various missions (Thompson 1982:7-10). Roth (1900:6) noted that 'payback' was evident among the "Koko-minni Aboriginals occupying the country drained by the middle Palmer River", bordering on Kuku-Yalanji country. Haviland and Hart (1998:75) write "witchcraft and the fear of revenge by witchcraft were pervasive in north Queensland Aboriginal society in the early part of the century."

Kunuth-Monks (1987:39) discusses the superstitions which often led to 'payback'.

> Among Aboriginal people, sickness and death were not perceived as being caused by germs and viruses, nor by any of the things to which we now know attribute sickness and death. They were caused, so they believed, either by someone manipulating the spirit world, someone who wanted to do them harm, or by

> someone using arangutia (evil spirits), or by having transgressed some tabu… often, innocent people were blamed and killed.

Thompson (1996:149) reports that sorcery was discussed at Lockhardt River when old people preparing for baptism

> came forward with various objects, each with its own superstitious settings, they showed a lively anxiety to put away old beliefs, and at the same time to readjust the intricate relationship laws (which had been a real stumbling block to their spiritual progress).

The Lockhardt River experience suggests that the people were concerned with some aspects of customary belief and discussed this with missionaries. Trigger (1992:204), writing about the Doomadgee mission in north-western Queensland, says that

> Aboriginal belief in sorcery had its counter-part within Christian doctrine… the missionaries' constant references to the way the Devil works in devious ways to generate the downfall of Christians were related easily by Aboriginal people to the spiritual forces believed to operate according to Blackfella law.

Roth (1900:21) recorded similarities between the Christian charcterization of the 'devil' and that of Aboriginal people near Mapoon when he noted "the soul or spirit of the dead" in reference to a story about "the devil outwitted by the human soul". The Kuku-Yalanji at Mossman describe the legend of "Wurrmbu, the flesh-eating demon, (who) had the body of a man, the wings of a flying fox, large pointy ears and teeth like a dog (Jakalbuku 1988, Erbacher 1991).

Recently, Yolngu elder, Djiniyini Gondarra (1996) declared the Northern Territory government euthanasia laws "an act of institutionalised sorcery". Social Darwinist aspects of early Assimilationist policy, e.g., eugenics and biological assimilation

-"the breeding out of colour" (R. Manne 1998:57) - might be simiiarly considered.

THE PASSING OF OLD YORKEY

In 1949, the Second World War had been over for three years and the Daintree Mission was busy building fences to house the new dairy cows. Fresh milk was distributed throughout the Mission. Jack Easton describes those days.

> I didn't know how to milk, so I had to learn that. We'd have prayers every morning. We'd hit the bell and let the people know. It was an old gas cylinder. Even when there was a big fog, the people would still come. Old Man Yorkey, Harry Shuan, Stumpy John, Charlie Crookleg, Willie Crosseye, Molly, Nellie Walker, Rosie Redheart, we'd all have prayers. Old man Yorkey came every morning. We'd have fellowship and share the Word.
>
> One morning, Old Yorkey said to the grand children and a few others, "I'm going walkabout today. I'm going over the river."
>
> "Alright Grand Dad, we'll come with you."
>
> "You won't," he said. "Stay here."
>
> He got into the boat and went over the other side of the river.
>
> Around about four o'clock in the afternoon, Norman Walker came to me.
>
> "Brother," he said, "Old Man Yorkey is not back and the people are concerned about him. Can we go and find him."
>
> We went down to the river and got a boat and went upstream. We saw his boat tied to a log. It was swamp country. We tied up and set out to find him. We kept going until we came to a big tree and there at the foot of the tree was Old Man Yorkey sitting there with his legs crossed, his old hat pulled down over his eyes. He was dead. He went over there to die. The boys who were with me started weeping. I joined in too. He was a good

> man. The Word says, 'Weep with those who weep and rejoice with those who rejoice.'
>
> I had the tear ducts rolling. We lifted him carefully and pulled out to the Mission. When we laid him out, the people started wailing there for some time. I let them go on into the night. Eventually I came over and said, "Why are you weeping so much?"
>
> "Old Man Yorkey was alone when he died," they said.
>
> "No, he wasn't. He was not alone. Someone was with him. Old Man Yorkey was always faithful in coming to the prayer meeting. I believe Yorkey in his own way loved the Lord and when he went out and died there, the Lord was with him. He wasn't alone. And now he's with the Lord."
>
> It stopped them weeping to the extent that they were. We had a funeral. I believe I'll see Old Man Yorkey in the Glory Land. I wouldn't have told a lie to those people just to stop them weeping. In their own way they loved the Lord and so we accept that. We don't look for perfection in them. What about the European? Do we ever get perfection in them? We're all full of faults and failings. The Lord understands all these things. He takes us just as we are. He knows our hearts. That's the same with a lot of the natives there. Praise the Lord.

Pastor Jack Goulder was known as the "Farmer-Missionary" at Daintree from Easter 1949 until he left for the Commonwealth Bible College, Brisbane in January 1953.

Ps. Goulder: One day I was talking to an old chap named Jimmy Walker. He said to me, "Brother, I love coming to church." We kept talking for a while and when I left him I started to think. Why would old Jimmy love coming to church because he was almost blind, he could hardly see. He was almost totally deaf. He doesn't have to come here to see the people. He can talk to them at any time in the village. He wouldn't be coming for the hymns or the singing because he couldn't sing anyway. He wouldn't be getting much out of the message if he heard it from where he used to sit? The only conclusion I could come to about Jimmy Walker was that he really loved the Lord. And that was why he came to church.

Ps. Westbrook: Did it take you long to learn the language?

Ps. Easton: Ah, sorry. We didn't learn the language. We learnt a few words, but we were flat out. We communicated through broken english, pidgin and different types of New Guinea. They were taught English in school. All the children could speak English well. Sister Davidson started the school at the Mission, then my wife Hazel carried on. When the children were growing up a bit, we used to take them up to the Daintree school. Then we had R.I. (Religious Instruction) up there. It was about five miles from the Mission to the school. We arranged literacy classes for those who couldn't go up to the school.

Now what about their culture? How did we treat them and their culture? Did we destroy all their culture? No. When I was up in New Guinea, we used to get the folk from the United Nations coming over every three years. A delegation. They used to ask questions and see how things were going. One of them asked me one day, "You're taking all the culture from the people. What're you replacing it with?" I said, "When we first came into this area, they were hating one another. They have different tribes and they had different clans and they were fighting one another. They were working sorcery against one another to destroy one another. We spoke against that in a nice way, not revoking them for the bad customs they had. We didn't say, "Don't do that!" We did it in a loving way. We were teaching them as the Lord came to manifest his love, to love one another, not to hate one another. And live peaceably one with the other. And so we were replacing their cultures of hatred and bitterness and enmity and replacing it with love and honesty and relationship.

And what were our attitudes towards the Aboriginals? And their coroborrees? We allowed them to have their coroborrees every Saturday night. And they manifested more energy in the coroborrees than when they were working. They used to have a coroborree digging stump holes. I used to watch them clapping boomerangs in their coroborrees and think 'they should do that during the week.' There was one thing we did do. At midnight, I was wide awake. I'd blow the whistle. They knew what it meant.

'Coroborree finished now.' They stopped and went peaceably to bed ready for church next morning.

We didn't condemn them because of their beliefs: 'Debil debil he stop along bush.' That was just what they'd been taught. We gently tried to explain that they were not there, saying, "And always remember, if the Devil's there, the Lord's there. And the Holy Spirit is there. God's angel's are there. You love the Lord! The Angel of the Lord encampeth around them that fear Him. And delivers them.'" (Psalm 34.7).

> We taught them the Word of God will do its own work. Quickened in their hearts by the Spirit. And will bring that to light not in the understanding which we've got - we're still learning aren't we? And yet we've been on the road so long, so you couldn't expect perfection from them. We sympathised with them. And we shared the Word with them. On Sunday afternoon, we used to go around and visit the families and sit down and share and talk in their homes.

Ceremonial life was also part of the mission experience at Yarrabah. Higgins (1981:17) mentions a 'native dance' as a send-off for the Aboriginal missionaries, James and Angelina Noble in 1904. Thompson (1982:28) says that during the 1970's at Lockhardt River mission, ceremonial life was accommodated within the working week. Easton's curfew on "coroborrees" is consistent with the Lockhardt River experience. Warby (1996:183) writes

> the Bora and Corroborees had been forbidden for many years and, with the passage of time, were in danger of being forgotten. Many old people had died and with them their intricate knowledge of their culture. Would I agree to them recommencing the Bora and Corroborees? I believed that this restraint, once imposed for reasons of the higher good of the people, could now be seen to be of the order of a cultural and spiritual tragedy. While they were Christians, they were very young Christians, and many of their ways inspired and served their people well for countless generations before Christ was born. Why should they not continue to do so? .... It is a vital means to their understanding of life and to their sense of identity. Rituals preserve our identity as a social group, but they also connect people through time.

Thompson (1982:12) writes of Mission life at Lockhardt River

> while much is valued in this social change, there are also destructive effects seen in the breakdown of authority, aimlessness, alcoholism and various disorders. Such lack of understanding and false views of Aboriginal society are themselves very disruptive to Aboriginal life. One particular false view expressed sometimes is the suggestion that the Bora (ceremony) includes the practice of sorcery. However, the activities of sorcery are related to conflict, not to the unifying aims of initiation ceremonies and have no place in them.

Amidst his daily superintending of the Daintree mission, Easton observed that there was little time for learning the Kuku-Yalanji language. The situation was similar at Oenpelli in the 1920's when Alf Dyer discovered that there was more than one language spoken on the mission. He had been "too busy surviving the immense problems of the isolated mission" to learn language (Harris, 1990:815).

Berndt (1988a:54) notes that "a considerable amount of linguistic and ethnographic information was recorded by early missionaries… it provides base-line data without which, some of us, and not least Aborigines, would be much poorer." Philip Jones (1988;150) notes that "missionary collections (of Aboriginal artifacts) were consequently the most comprehensive and best documented until the advent of investigative field anthropology in the twentieth century." The Kaurna language of the Fleurieu Peninsula (S.A.) is being revived, "based on the archives of the Kaurna and church leaders with whom they worked last century" (The Australian, 6/8/97). The pioneering Hermannsburg Lutheran missionary, Hermann Kempe (1844-1928), was a "most assiduous and successful student" of the local Aranda dialect and contributed several grammar and vocabularies in the Central

Australian language (Scherer, 1973:30). Such information gave missionaries, and later anthropologists, data for the rejection of Terra Nullius.

Ps Easton: One day, Johnny Chinley came rushing to me with his eyes sticking out like the headlights of a car. "Six big fella snake!" he said. "He stop long underneath leaves of the pineapple!" I said, "Go and kill them." They were death adders. Six of them.

Leila Gallienne: A carpet snake was given to the dormitory for the girls to eat. They cooked it and put a piece on my plate. No way in the world could I get that snake in my mouth.

Ps. Easton: No. I haven't had snake either. We had some poultry for eggs for the dormitory. Hazel was a lighter sleeper than me. She'd hear all the hens cackling. "Jack," she'd say. "Snakes. Wake up." I'd get out of bed, go to the door, grab the cane knife and go down to the shed where the chickens were. I put my nose up against the wire netting and here's the tail of a snake going right down beside my nose.

We were in the church service one Sunday morning and there was a lot of cackling going on. After the service, King Toby and the others walked over to the fowl house and of course, I took the cane knife with me. Here's a big 14' carpet snake with at least five chooks inside. Old King Toby walked off with the snake and they had a great feed off it. I wasn't afraid of snakes.

One time, Norman and I were cleaning out the shed we had for tools. I was going to put my hand over the top of this case and the Lord must have spoken to my heart. 'Don't put your hand in!' I said to Norman, "Give me a hand to get this case down." We lowered it down and here's this great big brown snake. We dealt with him.

Ps Goulder: Snakes weren't protected in those days.

Ps. Easton: We always had the midnight bus. Jimmy Martin used to bring the goods in on the Saturday afternoon and he'd pick up some of the natives from Mossman and when they got out of that truck they were like ghosts walking. You know what it was - the dust. They were like spirits when they arrived. But then in the night time, Saturday night was the only time they had the midnight bus. They'd come back home on the midnight bus and of course, I'd have to be up and awake and check them as they came out of the bus for drink. Never allowed drink on the Mission. They never tried to bring it either. We never had trouble with drink on the Mission.

Ps Westbrook: Could they come on the Mission if they were drunk?

Ps Easton: If they were on the midnight bus, yes. I wouldn't say, "Get out until you're sober!" No. I'd let them come on drunk. Let 'em go to bed. Sleep it off. We never had any fights as a result of them being drunk. Not that I can remember.

Ps. Goulder: No. There were no fights. There was some sweet clay between Daintree and the Mission on the left hand side of the road. They used to call it 'sweet clay'. They used to eat it because of the hookworm. The hookworm used to affect them. It used to make them nauseated inside and they used to go up the road and get this clay. It was only in a certain area between the Mission and Barrett Creek, and they used to eat it and get sick. Sick because they had all this clay inside them. So you had to get them into hospital so they could get cleaned out and get back to normal again.

One day, Daphne Watkins and Norman told Ps. Easton and myself that one of the children had been taken up the other side of the Daintree. We went up. It was just a little two year old baby. It was really stormy and heavy rain was falling. Daphne Watkins came with us. We picked the baby up and brought her into the Mossman hospital. She definitely would have died if we hadn't gone up and picked her up. They used to take the children away when they got sick, because they reckoned if they came to the hospital, they always blamed the system if the children died. But if the child lived after coming to the hospital then they said it was a result of their witchcraft. So you were in a 'no-win' situation. If the child died it was your fault. If the child got well, it was because of what they'd done. They'd always take the negative.

If the child died it was because the Mission took the child from us. It was a very hard thing to get over. A lot of children died because they had no medicine.

Ps Easton: There was a little exodus when I was there because the dogs were multiplying more than the people. I had to shoot some of the dogs. They were causing a lot of trouble in the village, so we had a meeting with the natives and said, "I'm going to relieve you of some of your pups." Stumpy John took off for Mossman with a string of dogs following him. He never returned, but something had to be done. The ground was full of hookworm. The children were walking around in the bush with excreta everywhere. We built pit toilets, but they wouldn't use them. First of all, they didn't have a pit toilet, they used to just go out in the bush and that was it.

The babies all got hookworm and were dying at an early age. Some of them told the children, "You no can go walkabout along toilets. You go in there, Devil Devil, he stoppim' in there long haul, you pullim' go down long haul. You finish true!" That stopped them using the toilets. We tried to help them all we could. Sure we did, but they were brought up in this other system. Hookworm was being treated by the Health Inspector from Cairns in conjunction with the health authorities at the hospital and you had to be sure the people got (Epsom) salts.

A dose of salts would have to sink down there in their intestines. I had to stand there with a stick. "You will not run away!" They ran away into the bush, but without the opening medicine it could kill them. I had to be the policeman. With a little persuasion, I got them to stay and take their salts. Shortly afterwards, I got malaria. The natives said, "Serve you right. You're getting punished now for killing our dogs." I survived.

Ps. Westbrook: Did you ever hit anybody with the stick?

Ps. Easton: Ah no. The Word says 'Lay hands suddenly on no man.' We never resorted to violence. We had no real discipline. Discipline was verbal. Love and compassion towards them, that's how we broke down a lot of barriers. Love breaks through all barriers.

Ps. Westbrook: Did you see many crocodiles?

Ps. Easton: Not many. The most I saw was in the hut one day when we were visiting. They had crocodile eggs in there and were hatching them. "What're you going to do with them?" I said. "Put them back in the river," they said. Put them back in the river!

Pastor Davidson gave each of the families a parcel of land to cultivate, but they didn't do anything with it. They were hunters. We cared for their health and they were all happy on the Mission.

> They used to wash the clothes down the river and never had any showers, but there was a spring up where brother Davidson had made a bit of a dam. Roily Ellis, who was in the Army, came up and brother Davidson got the pipes and built the temporary dam at the top of the hill and we reticulated the water right to the Mission. We dug the trench under the road and then built shower rooms at each end and washing facilities in the middle. We got the water laid on to the house too. Last time we were up, we went to find the cemetery they used on the Mission and we nearly got lost in the bush.

Prior to the coming of the Mission, a European school teacher, May Julia Cronen died at the mouth of the Daintree River and her body was brought up river and buried (June 13th, 1899) on the land which was later acquired for the Mission (1). Her grave was marked and surrounded by iron railings. This is the land later used as the Mission cemetery.

ENDNOTES:

1. QSA File No. 6Q/11. 4/1/1978. 5714.

Illustration 26. Newly weds at Daintree Mission, 1940s (Mossman AOG collection).

Illustration 27. Daphne Watkins and Daphne Dales with dormitory children at Daintree Mission, Clare O'Gilvie is at front on left, 1950 (Daphne Watkins collection).

Illustration 28. Daintree Mission 1946. L to R. Back row: Wilma Walker, Hazel Easton, Duncan Missionary, Daphne Dales. Billy Denman on far right. Mission church in background. (Mossman AOG collection.)

Illustration 29. John Goulder with 'Big Bertha', Daintree Mission in the late 1950s (Goulder collection).

Illustration 30. Ray Jackson with the dormitory children. Daintree Mission in the late 1950s (Mossman AOG collection).

CHAPTER SEVEN

1950–1959: BAPTISED AMONG CROCODILES

On the 8th September, 1949, the Mossman Protector, Sergeant R J. McNeven advised the Director that the Junction Camp near the centre of Mossman had been demolished.

> Mr. Eastern of Daintree Mission, Daintree came to Mossman with his truck and carted the natives and their property and huts from the Junction Camp to the Gorge Aboriginal Reserve, where they have taken up residence, with the exception of two who have gone to reside at Daintree Mission.
>
> I have visited the Gorge Reserve and pegged out the spots for huts to be built and assisted the natives to get accommodation arranged there, and all are now assisting in building nicer huts of a weekend and are quite happy in their surroundings.
>
> The Gorge Reserve has been laid out in a street, with huts each side with room to erect other huts as required. The surroundings have been cleaned up and with the regulation sanitary conveniences which were erected there some time ago the camp is now much improved in general.
>
> I took no active part in moving the aboriginals or their huts from the Junction Camp, but did give every assistance at the Gorge reserve after their removal.

The Protector advised the Director on 23rd March, 1950 that there were 27 permanent Aboriginal residents at the Gorge Reserve, 8 of whom were in receipt of 'indigent rations'.

> I… assisted the natives (at the Gorge) to peg out and build good huts from scrap galvanised iron, with thatched roofs, and each hut is 14' X 14' X 6' with hip roof, and all have built-in beds to keep the occupants off the ground, this combined with the installation by the Department of two sanitary conveniences has resulted in better health among the natives. The village is laid out in a street and is kept in a clean and tidy condition.
>
> To facilitate greater hygiene in the camp I have obtained a quote together with plans and specifications for the proposed erection of a single building containing two shower rooms, one for males and one for females, with a roofed and otherwise open washhouse at one side for clothing to be washed.

On July 1st, 1950, Pastor Jack and Hazel Easton left Daintree Mission for New Guinea. That week, the Gorge schoolteacher, Sister Dot Stennett died and Daphne Dales took up her post, assisting Ethel Vale. The late Dot Stennett's casket was on the train that carried the Eastons south.

The Assemblies of God (Qld) applied to erect a 'cottage' at the Gorge and on the 2nd November, 1950, the Protector advised

> Miss Ethel Vale is at present the Assemblies of God in Australia Mission Worker at the Gorge Aboriginal Reserve, Mossman. She resides in a very old bedraggled building which has an earth floor. A cottage is badly needed there, and I would recommend that favourable consideration be given to the request as outlined in attached letter.

A 'cottage' was subsequently built by the AOG (Qld). The framework cut to measure in Cairns and erected by volunteer labour using weather board milled at the Daintree Mission mill. The mill had been installed by Dudley Holland who replaced the Eastons, and manufactured 20 - 50 fruit cases required by the Mission each week. Those who helped build Ethel Vale's cottage included Ps Charles Enticknap, Norman Walker, John Goulder, Ps. Fred Lancaster, Hans Marbach and others. The Daintree Mission applied for permission to connect the telephone at the Gorge and twenty-five pounds was granted from the 'Vote-Special Missions Fund', provided that the mission supply the poles.

It appears that sometime in 1951, three years after returning from her three month holiday, Sister Ethel Vale departed the Gorge after more than twenty years of service. She was approaching her eightieth year. Meg Robinson and Daphne Dales were appointed as Missionaries at the Gorge whilst Daphne Watkins remained as dormitory matron at Daintree. Mr and Mrs Dudley Holland, who were superintending Daintree Mission, transported the children to Daintree School each day until Pastor Fred and Doris Lancaster arrived in December 1951 (9). Fred Lancaster was related to Mrs Sarah Jane Lancaster who had opened the Good News Hall in Melbourne in 1909. They had been pastoring the Assembly at Innisfail when they were invited to take over the superintendency of the Daintree and Gorge Missions and the Miallo Assembly, where meetings were held in the home of the Minniecons.

The responsibility of Mission maintenance can be seen in Warby's (1996:172) statement regarding the Anglican Lockhardt River Mission.

> In 1951 the State Government paid the Church of England Diocese of Carpentaria a meagre annual grant of 750 pounds to supplement the Church's voluntary outlay at Lockhardt River Mission. The Government also provided a basic weekly food ration per adult consisting of 71bs. of white flour, 1 lb. of sugar,

> with baking soda and cream of tartar, and lesser amounts for children. Malnutrition was commonplace. Following discussions with the Protector of Aborigines, Mr Con O'Leary, in 1952, the white flour was replaced by wholemeal flour. Molasses, golden syrup, peanut butter, hops and tinned milk were also provided, enabling porridge to be made from the wholemeal flour as well as bread and damper. The Church ran a few hundred head of cattle, two of which were killed each week and the meat was handed out to all families.

In 1952, the Deputy Director of Native Affairs wrote to the Under Secretary, Dept. of Health and Home Affairs, stating that the Assembly of God missionaries at Daintree Mission who were also supervising the Mossman Gorge Mission, were carrying out work "of considerable value where the welfare of aboriginals is concerned" (1). The Protector, W. T. Bartlam also informed the Director on 6th May, 1952 that the Daintree Mission "is well conducted ... The spiritual, moral and physical well-being of the natives are well cared for by the Mission authorities." However, on the 22nd May, 1952, the Director advised his Deputy

> Consistent with the previous discussions several years ago regarding status of the Daintree Mission, I am still not prepared to recommend a subsidy to this Mission until such time as it is determined that the area occupied by the Mission is handed over to the Government with no reservations. Until such time comes about it must be the policy of the Department to protect the aboriginals living there by giving to them the relief to which they are entitled and to see that the Institution Endowment is made available to the Mission, consistent with their care, protection and control of the children residing on the area.
>
> The question of a subsidy to the body as a recognised Mission can only be considered when this organisation operates on the same terms as other Missions, that is, that the land possessed

> by the organisation becomes an Aboriginal Reserve with no restrictions so far as the State Government is concerned.
>
> Meantime it is the function of the Native Affairs Department to inspect and examine the manner in which the area occupied by aboriginals is being conducted, particularly with reference to the care and welfare of the aboriginals and their general accommodation.
>
> It must be remembered that with the title of this land as it exists, no aboriginal person has legal right to erect a house at his own cost on the land. If such does occur, this building automatically becomes the property of the missionary body owning the land.

On the 29th July, 1952, the Deputy Director again wrote to the Under Secretary

> It is noted that this Mission has not been granted letters patent under the Religious Educational and Charitable Institutions Acts and it is presumed that such is what they now require. As the land on which this Mission is situated is not Crown land and is still owned by the Church, no Departmental subsidy is paid to this Mission. However, the Mission has done very good work amongst the aboriginals in the Mossman district and if the granting of the letters patent is advantageous to them it is recommended that such be arranged.

On September 29th, 1952, Native Affairs Departmental Inspector Davis reported that

> most of the (Gorge) natives work in and around Mossman and are able to keep themselves and their families from their earnings. Those unable to do so are issued with indigent rations by the Department through the Protector of Aboriginals at Mossman. The shower rooms and wash tubs provided last year are in good order and much appreciated by the resident natives. There are two lady missionaries residing on the Reserve, one of whom conducts a school for the children resident there.

Religious Instruction continued at the Daintree State School, staffed by teacher, Phillip Moody and Headmaster, Mr Douglas, Grace Crees, a descendant of one of the pioneer Daintree families and a teacher at Mossman Primary in 1997, attended Sunday School classes which were taught by Sisters Watins, Biddle and Ps Fred and Doris Lancaster who played guitar and piano accordion (11) under the Daintree State School between 1950 and 1954.

RG:	Grace, What do you remember about that time?
Grace:	I remember the chorus' we used to sing. I often join in with the kids at school. Some of them are still the same ones.
RG:	Did you go up to the Mission?
Grace:	Once or twice. I knew one of the girls, Kathleen Winkle. She used to be in our class at school and I got to know all the girls like that. A lot of kids came from the Aboriginal Reserve behind our property as well as from the Mission. We had a dairy farm at Daintree. My parents still live in the butter factory home next to where the caravan park is today. Our property was across the river and we had to row a boat to school. It was a two teacher school, the same one that's there today.

There was the old shop that was burnt down recently and the butcher shop next door. A bus used to run into Mossman and return with bread and mail. The different people of religion used to come out to Daintree. There was Catholic, Church of England and the Assembly of God chap who came to take all the others. We were Methodists. I taught Sunday School at the Daintree school when I was attending the Methodist Church, which became the Uniting Church in Mossman.

RG: What do you think about Religious Instruction in schools today?

Grace: It taught us the morals which are lacking today. We used to do activities as well. The kids still like colouring and Mrs Carter who comes here with the singing. It's good to see that still being carried on. We have HRE. Human Relations Education. We try and make students aware of other people's feelings - good and bad - and people who you can trust. They need that, because you don't know who you can trust in this day and age. So many children come from divided families. I don't think it's easy for a child to grow up these days. There's not a lot of role models. It all depends on the home life.

Reflecting on those days, Ps. Fred Lancaster writes

Early in our time I observed that all the workers were so busy and dedicated that both their own and the Mission's spiritual well-being was being affected. We arranged a meeting for all workers each Wednesday morning for workers on both missions. We had a Bible study, broke bread and had lunch together. The informal meetings were prayers first thing each morning and two services on Sunday (2).

At the end of 1952, fifty Aboriginal people were residing at Daintree Mission and there were twelve girls in the dormitory. Native Affairs Department Inspector Davis visited Daintree Mission accompanied by Sergeant Bartlam, the Mossman Protector. His report on the 29th September, 1952 notes

> The Mission adults reside in a number of poor quality galvanised iron huts with dirt floors and grass roofs. Arrangements are being made for the construction of better class houses for the people, the first of which is now in course of erection. A small sawmill on the property is providing the necessary timber. The Mission also has its own electric light plant which illuminates the church, dormitory, Superintendent's house and the camp area.
>
> About 10 acres are under cultivation, chiefly with bananas and pineapples. The sales of this fruit provide a large proportion of the mission's income. In addition potatoes, pawpaws and other fruit are grown for use on the Mission. The majority of the adult inmates are past working age; one is completely blind and another nearly blind. Very few of them would be capable of working under agreement outside the mission. Four of the men are employed by the Mission in the farm area and are paid wages and are issued with rations from Mission funds.
>
> The Mission is staffed by the Superintendent, Mr Lancaster and his wife who have one female and one male assistant. All are very keen on the work and the natives appear happy and contented. Any assistance which it is possible for the Department to give will, I am sure, be well worth while.

The sight impaired adult males referred to by Inspector Davis are almost certainly the late Charlie Denman Snr and his son Charlie, one of eleven children born at Greenhill Station near Archer's Point turn-off, Cooktown. Charlie Snr was a ringer on the station and sometimes resided at the Cooktown Reserve. Along with his brothers and sisters, they arrived at Daintree Mission in 1942 to join other family members already settled there. The Denmans had cataract blindness (8).

In January 1953, John Goulder left to attend the Commonwealth Bible College at New Farm in Brisbane. He was replaced by Ray Jackson, a school teacher from Victoria who had come to work in the Mossman Sugar Mill and became interested in the work at Daintree Mission. The Lancasters accepted a call to pastor the Woombye Assembly, but suitable replacement staff could not be found.

One of the last letters written by Ps Lancaster was to ask the Mossman Protector for financial assistance in constructing a replacement shed to shelter the weekly rations and clothing at the Gorge Mission. The original shed had been "constructed many years ago out of scantling timber and old corrugated iron, and … the earthen floor provides no protection from the rats or dampness." The Lancasters departed in September 1954 with Daphne Dales in charge of both Missions and Ray Jackson employed to supervise the Daintree farm. Approximately twelve Aboriginal workers were employed at the time as prices for bananas and pineapples were high and the acreage for both had been increased. This situation was maintained during 1955.

The AOG had trouble in finding suitably trained personnel to staff Daintree Mission. In a file note by the Deputy Director, dated 2nd December, 1954, he stated that on the 30th November

> Pastor F.A. Lancaster, until recently in charge of the Gorge and Daintree unofficial Missions, called with two of his Church leaders, Messrs. Wiggins and Moody, and discussed matters in connection with these Missions. Their Church is finding it difficult to find staff for both areas and the discussion

> concentrated around the transfer of aboriginals from the Daintree area to the Gorge....

In 1955, the Anglican parish in Mossman replaced its tin building known as St David's, and erected a stone building with stained glass windows on the original site where Dan Hart had first settled (3). Yarrabah and Lockhardt River were Anglican Missions. On the 12th November, 1955, the AOG wrote to the Deputy Director informing him that they recommended the transfer of Daintree Mission to the Gorge and were "desirous that your Department have due regard to the reactions and welfare of the natives concerned."

In 1956, the Queensland Lutheran Mission Board, which administered the Hope Vale Mission, agreed to take on the responsibilities of re-starting the mission at Bloomfield Reserve. There were approximately 130 Aboriginal people living on the river nearby (Anderson 1979:36).

On the 28th February, 1956, Ps. Lancaster advised the Deputy Director, Mr Richards

> Further to my previous correspondence re the possible moving of Daintree Mission activities to the Gorge Reserve, I wish to state that our Fellowship will not be taking any further action in this regard, owing entirely to the natives reticence towards such a move.
>
> We shall continue to appreciate what assistance your Department can offer for the general well-being of the natives on both missions.

The Cairns Regional Electricity Board set out terms for the connection of Mossman Gorge Aboriginal Reserve/Mission on 29th March, 1956. The government was now paying for the transportation of Daintree Mission schoolchildren to and from Daintree School each day.

THE NEW MISSIONARIES ARRIVE

Ps Henry Wiggins of the AOG State Executive visited Cairns and, became acquainted with Joe and Marjorie Cope. Originally from England, the Cope's were living with Mrs Cope's sister, while Mr Cope worked as a nurse at the Cairns hospital and Wiggins was staying next door. A conversation occurred in which they agreed to help out at Daintree Mission. Joe Cope was told to put it in writing. "Over the next few days, he wasn't sure if he had done the right thing and could get no rest" said Mrs Cope before they were accepted as missionaries to Daintree (4).

Daphne Dales was in charge and Margaret Biddle was dormitory matron when they arrived (5). A new electric generator was being installed by Leon Cook Snr. at the time (9). Marjorie Cope notes

> The folk waved us in and said, "Here comes Brother and Sister Goat. They didn't get the name, but it was lovely to see them. We had twelve dollars per week, but our dear Lord met the need. The folk were lovely and would not break bread if they did not feel right. We sometimes would say, talking like them, "Why you not take the Lord's bread?" They were honest and said, "We don't feel good inside." In some ways they could teach us white folk. They all came to church morning prayer and would pray in their way. Brother Cope got us all to read a verse of Scripture. We had 15 in the dormitory and we got two girls, Agnes and Gracie in Domestic Service in Cairns which we thought was great.
>
> During the early morning prayer meeting one day, Bro. Cope was worshipping the Lord and speaking in tongues. One of the young boys, Norman Walker the eldest of a family of ten, a lovely family, came up to him and touched him, saying that he was speaking in their language and was talking about the precious side of Jesus.

Every Wednesday, I had the village ladies out on the lawn, we had lovely grounds, and we had a meeting under the trees. We had singing, a little message and at the end, a cup of tea and cake. The shops in Mossman were very good to us. They sent in a tea chest of plain and self raising flour. There were a few weevils, but we got rid of them. The ladies took what they wanted and we had some. The Lord met our every need. The village folk went fishing and always gave us some, and I would give them some cake.

We had a box of clothing from one lady. As I took them out, something fell on the floor. I picked it up and it was a diamond ring. I put it safe and the next day I had a call on the phone asking if we had found it. The lady said it was her Mother's engagement ring and that she was now 80 and so upset about losing it. She wanted to buy us a winning (Casket) ticket, but I said, "No. It's alright, we don't believe in that."

One old man on the mission, named Jimmy, was failing. We tried to build him up with egg and milk rice pudding. He said, "Sister, me go home soon to my other home." I said, "No. We want you a bit yet." He replied, "By and by, I go to my home up there where grass is always green." He did, bless him. He knew where he was going. Charlie Denman was blind. He bought me a lovely wild yam one day. He asked me if I liked it and how I had cooked it. He told me to boil it but not to use any salt. A few days later, he said, "I've got another yam for you sister. This not wild one, this tame one." He had grown it. The people brought him to church. They were very stable folk.

The teacher at Daintree School, Phillip Moody was a Christian. We knew his parents. We took the Mission children to school and during this time the wife of the Headmaster, Mrs Douglas said to my husband, "Oh, Mr Cope. I don't know what's wrong with Charles. Will you have a word with him?" After talking, he knelt down and gave his heart to the Lord. They all started coming down to our little church at the Mission. A while later, Pastor Garrett came up from Cairns and all the family were

> baptized in the Daintree River. One old lady, Polly, was waving a branch around and chanting. "What are you doing, Polly?" I asked. "Chasing the rain away," she said, and funnily enough it did stop.
>
> We heard a noise in the chook yard one night. My husband said, "There's a snake, will you come with me and bring the torch?" Sure enough, it was up the tree with a chicken. My husband shot it. The next day, Polly and Rosy came and said, "Brother kill snake last night?" I agreed and they asked if two fellows could have it. I said, "With pleasure." Work boys took it and skinned it, cooked it and brought a bit on a plate. My husband took a little bit. They would share anything with us. If they killed a wild pig, they would bring us a leg. They said, "pigs eat our pineapples, we eat pig."
>
> Bread and meat came twice a week and was left at the mail box at the top of the drive. When we first went to Daintree, we had to serve out rations of tobacco, but in the latter years they were allowed their own pension. The younger men and women worked for different farmers. He would give them so much and the rest was paid into the Police. Sergeant Murray was a kind Protector. My husband took them into Mossman when they needed money. I did the medical treatment for the women and girls and he did the men and boys (6). Ray Jackson was a wonderful help with the two mission boys.

Ray Jackson lived in the Mission house. His father and sister Myrtle were regular visitors until he left to marry Evelyn Sirrup. In January 1957, Sister Biddle resigned and Alice Marbach took charge of the dormitory (9). Pauline Hollerhead assisted when Alice Marbach was on holidays. Marbach notes "those years were very busy, very absorbing, traumatic at times, and the things that claimed my attention were mostly day-by-day actual living… and the ups and downs of dormitory life" (10).

PRESERVATION AND SEGREGATION

At the beginning of 1957, the Office of the Director of Native Affairs moved back to Brisbane from Thursday Island after ten years of "post-war reorganisation" and the Deputy Director was posted to Thursday Island. On the 20th November, Dr. MacLurkin, the Medical Officer at Mossman wrote to the Minister for Health and Home Affairs drawing attention to conditions of general hygiene and hookworm infestation at the Mossman and Daintree missions

> For your information in 1954 there were 32 cases of hookworm notified; in 1955 - 32 cases; in 1956 - 34 cases, and this year to date there have been 37 cases. All these cases have occurred in aboriginal or native children. No cases have occurred amongst the white population.
>
> Efforts have been made to train the aboriginals in the Missions to use the conveniences supplied, but in spite of this, cases continue to occur. It would seem that the stage has now been reached where the whole of the ground in relation to the Missions must be polluted with the hookworm larvae.
>
> In the case of the Gorge River Mission in Mossman the overflow from the laundries etc. falls into a flat area close to the Mossman River. This area is swept by the floods in the rainy season and passes through Mossman. There have been several deaths among aboriginal children particularly in the case of babies....
>
> I fear that if these conditions are allowed to continue before long we will start having hookworm cases among the white population and possibly also some deaths.
>
> I note in Hansard 1957 page 316 in reply to a question from the Member for Kedron with regard to the Weipa Mission you replied that the policy of the Government was the protection and development of our aboriginals and complete assimilation of the aboriginal into the general community and that both from a humanitarian as well as a national point of view it is

> essential that our native people be not kept forever segregated as interesting museum pieces.
>
> Bearing these statements in mind I would respectfully make the following suggestions:-
>
> (1) To move the entire missions in stages to an area free from Hookworm after treating them individually before they go. After a lapse of three years they could return to the original missions. The original missions of course to be fenced off and barred for the period of three years.
>
> (2) The aboriginal children to be integrated into the community so that they can be trained in civilised hygiene. In the case of the Daintree Mission, the children already go to the local school; however, in Mossman this is not so. I would suggest that the children in Mossman be allowed to attend the local school where they can assimilate the basic hygiene principles.
>
> At present the aboriginals are living in most unhygienic and overcrowded dwellings. These in most cases are made of old black corrugated iron walls and thatched roof. Inside this they crowd together in large numbers and sleep in a number of cases on the floor and also light their fires inside the dwelling.
>
> If the Missions are not shifted then the alternative is that they must be rigidly trained in a higher standard of hygiene preferably by some government appointee. I feel very strongly that, although well meaning, the present representatives of the Church missions are totally unqualified for the task. Further, sufficient space must be provided between each building. The building must be surrounded by a fence and there must be a lavatory attached to each building.

The government continued to refuse financial subsidy to the Daintree Mission. The adult population on the 11th December, 1957, was 57 adults of whom 30 were children. Mr Bartlam, the Palm Island Superintendent added that sanitation was poor:

While the new lavatories were in good order - others in the area had cabinets with broken lids, or without lids. The two wash houses and back rooms were in a bad state and waste water ran to the side of the river and dispersed on the high sloping bank. The concrete floors were broken and holding pools of soapy water.

Housing: One cottage on stumps, with a wooden floor, has been constructed, and two have been commenced along similar lines. There is a sawbench run by an aged McCormick Deering Tractor on the Mission. The tractor also hauls the logs to the "Mill" for cutting into house timber. The remainder of the cottages are very primitive, being of smoke blackened and rusty iron, and with earth floors. The ground and homes were superficially tidy.

Schooling: The children go to the Daintree State School and ten (10) school girls and (1) one school boy are housed in the Dormitory which is a reasonably solid structure, but which requires minor repairs. A Dormitory Matron is in charge of this section.

Accommodations:

1. One (1) male and one (1) female bathroom, with two cubicles and showers in each, should be erected. Rubble drains to take the waste water should be constructed. Mr Cope has been informed of the need of these and the manner of their construction. He has agreed to keep in touch with Mr Baxter, Shire Council Health Officer, regarding these.

2. A number of cottages are required - at least five (5).

Following discussions with Mr Cope, Superintendent of the Mission, during which he stated the Mission could build the five (5) homes, and bathing and laundry facilities, with their own sawn timber if iron were provided, I recommend that 240 sheets of x 8' iron be granted to the Mission and authority to purchase up to 2 tons of cement locally for the erection of 5 cottages, and 2 bathrooms, 1 laundry and three (3) lavatory bases.

> 3. One set x 3 compartment concrete tubs are also required for the laundry.
>
> The work should be supervised, of course, by the local Protector, and any assistance should be carefully overseen.
>
> 4. The erection of three more lavatories, similar in type to those recently constructed, is essential.
>
> It is realised that the Daintree Mission is private property, but unless some realistic help is forthcoming, the position of the Native Residents will become increasingly difficult.

On 21st February, 1958, ten Aboriginal children from the Gorge were attending the Mossman State School. The Protector advised the Director

> there is no present transport scheme in operation for the conveyance. The matter of these children attending the State School was taken up with the Head Teacher, Mr Twedell, who informed me, that to date, he has received no objections regarding their attendance. They are arriving at school clean and tidily dressed and he is quite pleased with efforts at school.

Keith Hannah took over superintending at the Gorge on 1st September, 1958 and wrote to the Director about putting the

> river flat under vegetables and pineapples and bananas... as the Health folk up this way say the folk badly need fresh vegetables. We were wondering if you folk would help in any way with an implement, such as a small garden Rotary Hoe. I have spoken to the men about a garden and they are quite keen.

At the end of 1958, Joe Cope informed the Director that he had been ordered to stop building 'cottages' at the Daintree Mission by the Mossman Council, saying that he had been told to submit plans

> Thank you for the wash tubs which arrived and have been installed... We have completed 2 showers, one for ladies and

> one for gents and 2 wash places. We have explained to the natives that all this has come about as a gift from the D.N.A.

In his report of 22nd January, 1959, the Palm Island Superintendent acting on behalf of the Department of Native Affairs, wrote concerning the situation at Daintree

> One Native Cottage has been completed. It is 15' X 14' of two rooms. It has a wooden floor and is three feet off the ground. Council by laws call for 390 sq. feet of space exclusive of verandahs. However, this hut is a big improvement on the squalid shelter the occupants were previously living in. Mr Cope, Superintendent of the Mission, stated that the occupiers are not used to modern living quarters and that this was intended to be a big step in the right direction, and that he hoped they would progress to a stage where he could fit them for a bigger and more attractive home.
>
> I suggested to him that if he adds 10 feet to one side of each of the new homes he has commenced which would bring the area of each cottage to 370 sq. feet. However, Mr Cope has no knowledge of building and he has to rely upon Norman Walker, an aboriginal who works during the week and is only able to assist on Saturdays. His assistance involves the hauling in and milling of logs and erection of the cottages/laundries, showers etc.
>
> The hauling will have to be done in future with a borrowed tractor as the Mission one is immobilised with wheel bearing trouble and can only be used as a source of power at the Sawmill. The quality of the work is not tradesmanlike but an effort to make the buildings as strong as possible is noticeable. Frankly, I am of the opinion that unless some real help in labor and material is given to the Mission it will be a long time before the houses are erected, with the tractor broken down and labour reduced to one man for one day per week.
>
> I agree with Mr Cope that larger houses will only tend to congestion as the people like to crowd together with closed

> windows and doors if permitted. Would you please advise whether the Mission is bound strictly to conform with building regulations of a local authority.

However, the following month, on 10th February, 1959, the Director wrote to Ps. Lancaster in his capacity as General Secretary of the Queensland Conference of the Assembly of God in Australia.

> Over recent months criticisms against living conditions, of aboriginals on your Daintree Mission have been received at this Office. The health authorities in Mossman appear to be dis-satisfied with your Accommodation arrangements and although the Department has provided some assistance in an endeavour to reasonably meet the situation, such still does not fulfill requirements.
>
> The status of your Mission at Daintree is quite appreciated here. Briefly the position is you have established a Mission for which you are solely responsible in that it is not an aboriginal Reserve and no subsidy as provided for a recognised authorised Mission is paid by the Government. It is felt that the position now warrants a conference between your representatives and the Director of Native Affairs in the very near future to determine a policy better than applies now with respect to this Mission. Will you please advise if you or some responsible representatives are prepared to attend such conference in approximately two weeks time when the Director will return from recreation leave.

A copy of the letter containing details that had been known to the Department for almost ten years, was forwarded to Mr Cope at the Daintree Mission and to the Superintendent at the Palm Island Settlement. The AOG again offered to transfer "8 - 10 acres" of the Daintree Mission to the government provided that

> the land was used as a Reserve, the AOG be permitted to continue to have the spiritual oversite of the Natives, it did not

> involve the AOG in greater financial commitment than that with which they were currently obligated and that the necessary housing was erected upon the land being transferred... but we are not interested in transferring land if nothing more is to be done for the Natives than has been done at the Gorge Reserve where the conditions are no better than on the private land at Daintree.

The Director advised the AOG on the 12th May, 1959, that they would excise 12 to 14 acres including the dormitory, but excluding the Superintendent's residence and the Church. The cost of erecting five 'cottages' was given as 3,250 pounds. No subsidy was being paid to the AOG for their work at the Gorge Reserve as it was recognised as an 'unofficial Mission'. The government at this time was in two minds as to which course of action to follow. They appeared dis-satisfied with conditions at both the Daintree Mission and the Gorge Reserve.

In 1959, Aboriginal men and women gained the 'old-age' pension (Thompson 1996: 156) and in mid-year, after four years at Daintree Mission, Joe and Marjorie Cope went on leave. Ps Jack and Yvonne Goulder cared for the Mission for three months during which time the Cope's resigned. They went to Yungaburra for two years and continued to help out at the Gorge Mission. Roy Listing is also mentioned as being involved at this time. Ruth Becker, took over at Daintree Mission when the Goulders went to New Guinea and Ps Keith and Dawn Hannah came over from the Gorge, assisted by the late Ruth Dayman (nee Becker) and Esther Luscombe until Brian and Elva Day arrived at the beginning of 1960 (7). The Hannahs moved back to the Gorge, where the Department of Native affairs had constructed six new houses for Aboriginal occupation. A private citizen, Mr Raymond D. Rex O.B.E., notified the Director on January 12th, 1960

> it was pleasing to see the vast improvement. To see the new houses complete and well equipped costing 750 pounds each which were most generously granted by your Department, indeed, an admirable monument to the policy of your Government for the interest regarding the upliftment of the lives of our Aboriginals.
>
> I find in Mr Hannah, a man of integrity as its Missioner and full of appreciation towards our Natives and quite ready to do more if helped. He is an erstwhile farmer and can do the job. The village of 69 souls made up of 38 children - some in arms and some about to deliver and occupying up to school age. Those of school age are taken to Mossman State School by Mr Hannah's private truck.

Inspector Draffin recommended the purchase of a mower or rotary hoe and the clearing of a sports field as well as a cow paddock. The cows were to be provided from the Daintree Mission herd, but a major change was imminent.

ENDNOTES

1. Qld State Archives (QSA). 10/10/52.
2. Ps. Lancaster letter to author 8.5.96.
3. Mossman Gazette. 2/10/97. p. 10.
4. Marjorie Cope letter to author 9.4.96.
5. Daphne Dales was at Daintree when Isabella Hetherington died in 1946 She went to help Ethel Vale at the Gorge. Daphne Dales was in charge at Daintree when the Cope's arrived in 1956, a total of at least ten years service at both Missions. (Florence) Daphne Dales passed away, New Year's Day, 1972. She was from the Mundubbera, Gayndah area of S.E. Queensland.
6. Joe and Marjorie Cope were married 57 years. Mr Cope died in 1993. Mrs Cope is retired in Nottinghamshire, England.
7. Letter to author from Elva Day. 23/9/96.
8. 'Coming Home after fifty years.' Cooktown Local News.

24/3/93:13.

9. Letter from Dawn Parker to Ps Westbrook. 8/10/95.
10. Alice Marbach letter to author. 31/5/96.
11. Grace Crees interview with author. Mossman. December. 1995.

Illustration 31. Ps Lancaster baptising in the river 1950s (Lancaster collection).

Illustration 32. Marjorie and Joe Cope with Myrtle Jackson, Daintree Mission 1956 (Mossman AOG collection).

Illustration 33. Arthur and Mary Diamond wedding, Daintree Mission 1951. L to R standing: Mr and Mrs Holland with Daphne Watkins and the Mossman Police Sergeant (Mossman AOG collection).

Illustration 34. Dormitory children with Mary Diamond. Front row on left: Agness Mossman (dec), Clair O'Gilvie, Kathy Morris (dec.). Back row: Wilma Toby, Alice Shuan (Mossman AOG collection).

Illustration 35. In front of Daintree Mission house, 1950. Farewell to Jack and Hazel Easton. L to R: Ps Stan Douglas, Mrs W. Enticknap, Ps and Mrs Holland, Ps Will Enticknap, Ps Jack Easton (Mossman AOG collection).

Illustration 36. Jimmy Mossman, Daintree Mission, March 1954 (Mossman AOG collection).

CHAPTER EIGHT

1959–1962: MOVING ON

Towards the late 1950's, the AOG began appointing missionaries to the New Guinea field and approached the Department of Native Affairs for financial assistance at Daintree. In April 1959, Inspector Draffin from the Department of Native Affairs in company with the Palm Island Superintendent, Mr Bartlam, was considering excising 15 acres from Daintree Mission as a Reserve and constructing 'native homes' utilising Aboriginal labour from Palm Island, however, this did not come to pass.

On the 15th September 1961, Ps Lancaster called on the Director in Brisbane, advising that the population in the Daintree district was dwindling. The Butter Factory had closed and the area was changing from a small farming area to beef cattle. Ps Lancaster considered that employment opportunities for Aboriginals in the area were diminished, and, apart from small fruit sales in Mossman, the nearest avenue for sales of small crops was seventy miles away in Cairns. The Director noted that when the Protector obtained employment for Aboriginals they moved to the Gorge Reserve and that numbers were dwindling on Daintree Mission.

The Aboriginal population at Daintree Mission on 26th September 1961, was reported by Inspector Draffin to be 20 adults and 29 children.

> Of the adults, eight are employed and eight are Pensioners. Of the children, seventeen are of school age. Of the eight adults employed, five could be accommodated with their employers and there may be a possibility of the remaining three being similarly accommodated. These people are employed in close proximity to Mossman. … It is recommended that the people now resident on Daintree Mission be gradually transferred to the Gorge Reserve as accommodation is provided. Mr Hannah (Gorge Mission Superintendent)… confirmed that he would be able to construct accommodation similiar to that recently erected by the Department of Public Works and could produce the timber on a saw bench owned by the Mission. All that would be required would be builders, hardware and cement.

Ps Lancaster stated that "his committee felt that under the circumstances it was not sound finance to put further money into Daintree, but that the best arrangement would be to transfer all the Daintree natives to the Gorge." Ps. Lancaster remembers, "they (the State government) proposed sending all the natives to the Anglican Mission near Cairns (Yarrabah), but we suggested combining the two Missions into one establishment on the 43 acres of government Reserve at the Gorge. They agreed and began erecting new huts."

The recently arrived Mossman Protector, Mr Booth, advised the Director on January 2nd, 1962, that Mr Hannah, who was to mill and provide the timber himself, had approached him for the hardware and cement.

> At present there are two wash tubs for use by 85 natives and with the additional transfer of approx. 45 natives from Daintree Mission these will not be enough. I respectfully request that 6 additional wash tubs be supplied… and further, could the respective natives, funds permitting, obtain and have installed inside kitchen sinks?

> Sir, it will be appreciated that I have only taken this Office on the 18th December, 1961 and any information regarding the building plan for the natives at this Reserve will be appreciated. With regard to Mr Hannah, it would appear that he had dedicated his life to the Natives within this district, he is only in receipt of three pounds per week for himself and his wife (each) and he has asked me if there is any way by which the Department would appoint him a Mission Superintendent to the Gorge Mission at Mossman. He would resign from the Assembly of God but would still conduct his own service for the natives. This in my opinion is what is urgently required by the natives in this District. It would greatly assist me and also your Department for the good of all Natives within this District. As the matter now stands he has no authority over them whatsoever, but if appointed as a Mission Superintendent and paid by the D.N.A., he would greatly assist your office and mine.

However, within six months Brian and Elva Day from Daintree had replaced Keith and Dawn Hannah at the Gorge. The Protector noted that Mr Day had no vehicle to convey the children to school, that a new truck should be purchased by the Native Affairs Department for that use and advised that the timber on the Reserve could be sold to meet its cost.

> I have made inquiries at Mossman and have been advised that there is at least over 3,000 pounds worth of good timber on the Aboriginal Reserve… With reference to the transfer of the Daintree Mission to Gorge Mission, I have to advise that as the matter now stands, at least 5 new huts are required before the transfer can take place. I have contacted all Aboriginals in this regard and they are only too willing to pay for their own homes and to be moved to the Gorge Mission as soon as possible.

On 5th July, 1962, the Director notified his Deputy on Thursday Island that the AOG had "recently… advised that arrangements for closing down of Daintree Mission had been completed and that the families had transferred to the Gorge." Correspondence between the Director and the Mossman Protector on 6th March, 1962 shows that Draffin's recommendations to close the mission had been accepted as departmental policy. The Protector noted on 10th July, 1962 that "over a period of time there has been a large volume of natives calling at this office requesting exemption from the provisions of the Aboriginals Preservation and Protection Act." He devised a system whereby Aboriginals could draw on their bank accounts against food orders drawn up on their behalf by the 'Missionary in Charge of the Reserve' at local stores, assisting them to purchase blankets and provisions for the new homes at the Gorge.

In 1961, "the Act" still intervened in the lives of Aboriginal people (Anderson,1989:76). This was five years prior to the 1967 referendum in which 92% of Australian voters approved giving the Commonwealth powers to make laws enabling Aboriginals to vote in Federal elections and be counted in the Census. On 26th September 1962, the Mossman Shire Clerk wrote to the Director of Native Affairs thanking him for making Inspector Draffin available to answer questions and assuring them that "applications by aboriginals from the exemption of the Act will be thoroughly investigated before their release is granted… (with regard to) housing and employment."

The Deputy Director observed in a memo dated 5th July, 1962 that they were fortunate in having Sergeant Booth, "who has shown a much greater interest in the promotion of aboriginal welfare than his predecessor…". The need for an Aboriginal Affairs bureaucracy can be seen in the increased paperwork for the Protector. The government was now forced to manage a situation that had arisen from paternal policy.

On the 8th September 1962, the Daintree Mission was auctioned (2). There has been some controversy over the closure of the Daintree Mission. Some Kuku-Yalanji have argued that the situation should have been negotiated with them, before they were given the option of re-settling at Mossman Gorge. There is also Protector Booth's January 2nd, 1961 correspondence mentioning that the Daintree residents were willing to purchase their own homes and move to the Gorge as soon as possible.

Reasons given for the closure of Daintree Mission are varied. Alice Marbach, who had been in charge of the Daintree dormitory for the past five years (January 1957 - April 1962) notes

> the reason given officially was that it was not economically reasonable to have two missions so close together. The people of both missions were of the one tribe and most of the available work for the men was in the cane growing fields around Mossman. At about that time, there began to be, in government circles, plans to end the dormitory system. The children were returned to their parents (3).

Thompson (1996:157) says that around 1960, "the Queensland Government became critical of the achievements of Church Missions, but strong defences were made and the abysmal under-funding of them was revealed when it was admitted in parliament that a takeover of Church Missions would cost the Government 1.25 to 1.5 million pounds a year."

Twenty-one girls and five boys ranging in age from four to 18 years passed through the Daintree dormitory. Employment was found in Cairns for Grace, Agnes, Kathleen Winkle, Bella Brown, Doreen Winkle and Teresa Kookoe. When the Mission closed, the younger children went to their parents while others were cared for under the supervision of the Gorge Mission staff at the direction of the Department of Native Affairs.

The Port Douglas and Mossman Gazette (23/12/86) quoted one Kuku-Yalanji woman as saying

> My people lived in the Assembly of God mission in the Daintree and this land was sold under our feet by the church to build a new church in Brisbane. The police came with batons and guns and threw us into wagons with chains on our hands and feet. They burnt down our grass huts which were spotlessly clean, and herded us up like animals. We were brought to the Gorge Mission but always wanted to go back to our tribal lands north of the river.
>
> Many of the old people from the Daintree Mission died of a broken heart and today not many remain to tell the story of these times. I was 18 at the time and remember it well. We were so frightened and crying in the paddy wagons we did not offer much resistance. We came to stay with relatives at the Gorge until houses were built to accommodate us.

Ps Jack Easton has argued that if this story is to be accepted as fact, then surely the Protector would have given the Missionary some latitude as had been demonstrated in the move from the Junction Camp to the Gorge. Ps Keith Hannah, who with his wife Dawn had spent seven years at Mossman and Daintree, their two children being born there, writes

> The report is filled with fanciful imagination. There was no big drama at all, although there was much sadness at leaving Daintree, the shift to Mossman was very ordinary. The police never took part. It was carried out over a few weeks, moving one family down at a time. I built the houses at the Gorge. I went to the Government, (the Department of Native Affairs) and spoke to them of conditions and what could be done. They gave me permission to mill the timber from the Gorge Reserve which I did, supplying my own mill from our farm at Woombye. The

Government supplied the roofing, fibro and cement etc. The Walker family were left at Daintree for a period as caretakers until the sale went through. The cane farmer who purchased the Mission property and who had a cane farm just down the road from the Gorge, took possession and bulldozed the old village and he prepared his land to plant cane (4).

Wilma Walker, who gained exemption from "the Act" in 1961, recalls the move to Mossman.

RG:	When the Daintree Mission closed did you come to the Gorge?
Wilma:	No. It was full. I still had my house at the Mission. My husband and I were the last ones on the Mission. There was nobody else living there for a long time. My husband got a job at Daintree town. Then he got a job with Mr Jack cutting cane. My boys were cutting cane. We were waiting for an answer from the Department about a house in Mossman, then I came here (Mossman), but my husband was still up at Daintree Mission working for that farmer.
RG:	Did the police come to take the people to the Gorge and burn down the huts?
Wilma:	I was the last one there. Me and my husband and the boys and Gerry Douglas. He said, "I'm shifting now." My husband helped him with the truck. They didn't ask us. We dug that road through to the bananas.
RG:	Were you going to church after the Mission closed?

Wilma: Yeah. In Daintree town with that Christie. Tuesday or Wednesday night in the hall. Mr and Mrs Christie from Mossman Methodist Church. It used to be across the road from the newsagent. When the people came back to the Gorge from the Daintree Mission, they all died. There was no fishing. They had a good time up there, working there.

You know that Duncan Missionary? That's Barney's son. He used to go with Bella Ellington's mother. Bella born up the Gorge. Duncan got land for the aboriginal people up at Daintree, across the river there. Called Wowal Dimbi. Long time ago he got that before he died.

I've got five boys and five girls. One died at Daintree. He's the baby born in a gunyah. All the old people was there. They delivered the baby. My son, Kevin Walker, we put him in the dormitory because we couldn't look after him without the medicines. He's working in Mossman now. Bennett lives at Cooya Beach.

I used to tell my kids about Jesus. They won't listen, but they know. I used to take my kids to Sunday School. They used to go to church and all that. I said, "You must get girlfriend in church," but they said no. I always pray. The Lord look after me everywhere I go.

Norman Mitchell, an Aboriginal born at Mt Molloy, 30 miles west of Mossman in approximately 1920, became a Christian around 1950 (7). Mitchell spent some time at Mossman Gorge during the 1960s.

> I used to preach the Gospel at Mossman Gorge and travelled widely through Cape York. I met a teacher bloke. He came from Dutch. He learned the (Kuku-Yalanji) language which gave the Aboriginal people more influence toward God. He was a Dutch American. He was a very classical person. He got to the very tap root of our language. He stopped there eleven years at Bloomfield, preaching and teaching among the people.
>
> That was hard to believe, to find a white man preaching and teaching in the same language. Let me tell you, he was pretty good in Kuku-Yalanji. He got a Bible and translate it. I don't read it, but I can read it by thoughts, understand it, the meaning. Those people there in Mossman, they were quick to pick up the language and they heard from Mr. Hank Herschberger, preaching, teaching 'round Rossville, Daintree and Mossman. I learnt much more of the language, how to get about everything OK. The attraction of the Word, its story, how to get its meaning and the wondrous of the wonder, story went on.
>
> This Hank wrote some hymn book in Kuku, in the language, wrote many stories belong to our people, Kuku-Yalanji. (5)

Lena Oui (nee Pitt) was born in Port Douglas in 1928. Her father was born on Murray Island and her mother at Yarrabah. Her parents attended St David's Church of England in Mossman. Lena was twelve years old when her parents moved to Daintree. The family lived outside the Mission on the Daintree Road, but went to the Mission church as well as to services held at the Gorge (6).

> RG: Lena, after the Mission closed and moved to the Gorge, where did you go to church?
>
> Lena: I was a Sunday School teacher at the Gorge.

> Ps. Enticknap was coming in and out all the time. He'd come for a little while, stay up in the Mission house and go again. After Daintree finished, a lot of them would still come to our place once a month, but some of them more or less gave it away. It's a hard walk when you're on your own, but I'm not going to sit down and worry about myself. Me, I've got nothing, but I've got the Lord. I want to go where he makes a way for me, but we coloured folk were brought up to be asked.

FREEDOM FROM THE ACT

In February 1968, the Department of Aboriginal and Island Affairs in Cairns wrote to the Director in Brisbane advising of "European public feeling in Mossman (in) reference to Aboriginal people in general and Mossman Gorge and Lockhardt River people in particular". They were concerned about the "nightly fights" and "generally disorderly conduct" in Mossman. The Anglican minister, Rev. Atkins complained of "public drunkeness, loud swearing and brawling in the town centre not occasionally, but daily". It was felt that the Department of Aboriginal and Island Affairs should take over the control of the Mission.

Brian and Elva Day left the Gorge after six years in November, 1967 and Mrs Barrett, a widow, was subsequently appointed. There were approximately 120 people residing at the Gorge Reserve/Mission. The Protector advised on the 23rd February, 1968

> now that they (the Aboriginals) are entitled to drink… liquor is being taken into the Mission at will… . The working men work an average of four months per year and the rest of the time

> they will not work as they are in receipt of Social Services and most of this money is being spent on liquor and very little food is obtained and the Aboriginals at the Mission are living like parasites.... at the present they are unable to understand their own position and are in need of guidance and control.

As a result of full citizenship rights inferred in the 1967 Referendum, the Kuku-Yalanji could legally consume alcohol, but they had no control over development on their ancestral land. The result of alcohol abuse, including cross-cultural, intrafamilial and intergroup conflict, revealed that the terms of Assimilation were unsuccessful.

ENDNOTES

1. Ps. Fred Lancaster letter to author. 8.5.96.
2. Letter from AOG State Clerk to author 8 /11 / 96.
3. Alice Marbach letter to author. 23.7.96.
4. Keith Hannah letter to author. 16.7.96.
5. A translation of the Book of Acts into the 'Gugu-Yalanji' language was made by members of the Wycliffe Bible Translators with help from the people of the Bloomfield River area. The text was checked by the Translation Department of the Summer Institute of Linguistics, Australian Aborigines Branch, underwritten by Scriptures Unlimited, South Holland, Illinois, U.S.A. and published in 1972. A copy was on display at the Gorge Community shop in 1996.
6. Lena Pitt interview with author. Mossman. 28/11/95.
7. Norman Mitchell interview with author at the Fred Leftwich Retirement Home. Mareeba. 6/2/96.9/2/96.

Blood Relatives (if Single) other than Parents
(Required for Estate Purposes)

NAME	RELATIONSHIP	PROTECTORATE

Marks, Scars, &c. Nil

Signature of Aboriginal

(This is required in every case where Aboriginal can sign his or her name)

Witness to Signature or Thumb Print [signature] Protect

Right Thumb Print.
A clear, legible, rolled print is required in every case whether Aboriginal can write or not.

Left Thumb Print.

Govt. Printer, Brisbane (K)

Illustration 37. A Protectors' paperwork

1:1-3 1

1 1 Theophilus, ngayu jakalbaku yunundu
kaban yungan. Yinyaymba kabanba
ngayu yunundu balkan Jesus wanjarrmalmanda.
Ngayu balkan nyulu janangan wanyurrinku
balkan-balkan, binal-bal-ban. Nyulu yalakuda
balkan-balkankuda. 2 Wawu yinyamun nyulu
wangkar-wangkar-bungajin, heavenba-bungajin.
Nyulu heavenba dunganjiku, nyulu jawun-karra
12-bala wangkanin. Nyulu kuku dajin jananda
jawun-karranda 12-balanda balkanka jana
wanjarrmanka. Nyulu jananda kuku dajin
Godundumundu Wawubu junkurrdu. 3 Wawu kukumun
Jesus bajay-bajayman, warrngkal-warrngkan,
wulanyarrkuda, yarkinmanyarrkuda. Yinyamun
nyulu juranman baja. Nyulu 40-days jawun-
karranda 12-balanda jururr-jururr nguwimal-
milbijin, wubul junjuy-junjuy balkan, bama

---

1 Dear Theophilus:
In my first book I wrote about all the things
that Jesus did and taught, from the time he
began his work 2 until the day he was taken up to
heaven. Before he was taken up he gave instructions
by the power of the Holy Spirit to the men he had
chosen as his apostles. 3 For forty days after his
death he showed himself to them many times, in ways
that proved beyond doubt that he was alive; he was

Illustration 38. The New Testament in Kuku-Yalandji, 1970s.

CHAPTER NINE

POSTSCRIPT

The closure of the Daintree Mission in 1962 coincided with an era of significant political change for the Kuku-Yalanji. After the 1958/1964 Yirrkala dispute regarding bauxite mining leases awarded by the government to Comalco (Wells, 1982), there was an appreciation that Aboriginal people had not abandoned the desire to regain autonomy over their traditional land. Since 1960, governments began to administer reserves formerly administered by church bodies as missions. Under the new arrangement, public servants occupied staff housing and alcohol came into the community. The installation of liquor outlets had a devastating effect (Hunter, 1993; d'Abbs et al, 1994; Thompson, 1982:12), contributing to a breakdown in eldership authority and tradition (Thompson, 1982:12; Erbacher, 1991; d'Abbs et al, 1994). Gondarra (1993) notes

> money and other things were coming into the community from the government. The people became more rich and were handling lots of things such as motor cars, T.V., motor boats, and good houses. The responsibilities were in the hands of the Aboriginal people and no longer in the missionaries' hands.

Deductions from wages for the cost of Reserve maintenance continued until the Queensland Aboriginal and Torres Strait Islanders Act in 1965, when the office of Protector was transferred from police to civilian supervision with the Clerk of the local court made District Officer under one of three Regional Officers throughout the State. Aboriginal issues in Queensland gained portfolio status as Conservation, Marine and Aboriginal Affairs in September, 1969.

In 1971, at the Mossman Gorge Reserve which was still an unofficial mission, Ps Willie Enticknap was assisting when Ralph and Elsie Kajewski arrived. They spent two years ministering there and in that time

> the Gorge church tithes went up from $7 per fortnight to $70 per week. Seven people were baptised in the Spirit, coming right through until they were flowing in tongues and Lorna Toby was healed of an enlarged heart through prayer.

In 1973, Mr Taylor, one of the last AOG missionaries at the Gorge, departed and the Mission was handed over to the Australian Inland Mission (A.I.M.) (2).

SELF-DETERMINATION AND LAND RIGHTS

In December, 1974, the portfolio of Aboriginal and Islander Advancement combined with the Water Resources portfolio in the Bjelke-Petersen National/Liberal government. Federal Legislation for Land Rights was being drawn up by the Whitlam Labour government in Canberra. Ps Wes and Ethel Caddy had a teaching mission at the Gorge when the A.I.M. departed, due to a tragic accident involving a young Aboriginal man who was run-over whilst laying on the road at night by two women missionaries (3). The Church of Christ then began missionary work at the Gorge.

The Whitlam government enacted the Racial Discrimination Act (RDA) of 1975, which was the first Commonwealth law dealing with discrimination. It could override State laws and was to be an influential Act in assisting Aboriginal people to overcome the institutionalised attitudes that were prejudicial to their cultural independence (Antonios, 1995). Self-Determination replaced Assimilation as federal policy during the Whitlam government 1972-75 (Antonios, 1995:886). In 1976, the Fraser Liberal/National government passed the Labour initiated Aboriginal Land Rights (N.T.) Act 1976 in modified form (the clause that gave mineral rights on claimed land was removed. It is arguable that benefits flowing from these royalties may have contributed to an improved economic and social outcome for Aboriginal people and the State). Brennan (1998:165) writes "land rights is now legally classifiable as the restitution, recognition and compensation of property rights."

The Department of Native Affairs removed Aboriginal residents from the Old Mapoon Mission in favour of bauxite mining leases granted to Comalco in 1956 (Howitt, 1998) and on November 21, 1975 announced plans for a bauxite mine adjacent to Aurukun. Brown (1999:25) notes that on March 13th, 1978, the Queensland government "moved to take direct control and management" of Aurukun (Wik Munkan) and Mornington Island, two Aboriginal 'communities' in Cape York. The Presbyterians had administered these 'communities' for most of the century as an agency of the State government and now as the Uniting Church, "had taken significant steps to transfer to the two communities leadership in and control of all areas of decision making concerning their community life".

Referring to Land Rights, Brown (1999:31) writes

> the movement is important also for the growth of the Aboriginal Church, as Christian people work through what it means for them to baptize their culture into Christian faith, and to be Aboriginal Christians, Christian Aboriginal people... the vision... is that of a kingdom 'from every nation, from all

> tribes and peoples and tongues, standing before the throne and before the Lamb... and crying out with a loud voice, "Salvation belongs to our God who sits upon the throne, and to the Lamb'" (Revelation,7:9-10).

Towards the end of the 1970s, the Brethren replaced the Church of Christ as missionaries at the Mossman Gorge. A remnant of Pentecostal Christians had remained within the Mossman community and Ps. Roy Braike began Outreach meetings in the CWA Hall on Saturday nights. The Assemblies of God at Mossman began regular services again when Ps Albert and Dianne Van Zoggel arrived in November 1981. By April, 1982, "between 25 and 40 people were attending the Saturday night and Sunday morning services. Seven baptisms had been performed and many healed in Jesus' name" (4). There were now over 222 Assembly of God churches throughout Australia (5).

SOCIAL NEEDS

Land Rights legislation had jurisdiction in S.A. and the N.T., where the Country Liberal Party government contested the issue in the courts. In Queensland, The 'Land Act (Aboriginal and Islander Land Grants) Amendment Act' was passed, providing for the transfer of reserve land to incorporated Aboriginal Community Councils under a Deed of Grant in Trust (DOGIT). Recognition of the need for land title did not remove the underlying emotional and psychological problems of dispossession (Reser 1990:52). Alcohol was still a major problem within Aboriginal communities. In 1987, a Royal Commission into Aboriginal Deaths in Custody found that most were intoxicated at the time of their arrest.

In 1983, Martin Hovey was called to the AOG Mossman as a full time Pastor, completely supported locally, with 30

- 35 adults regularly attending meetings. Ps. Arthur and Elaine Westbrook took over the Mossman AOG fellowship in 1987 and began a Missionary program known as Frontier Evangelism with initiatives throughout Cape York and the Torres Strait Islands. Labor came to government in Queensland in 1989 and enacted the 'Queensland Aboriginal Land Act 1991', which allowed Aboriginal people to claim land outside the boundary of a Reserve, but only that which the government declared available. On June 3rd 1992, in Eddie Mabo v The State of Queensland the High Court of Australia declared "the lands of this continent were not terra nullius or 'pracically unoccupied' in 1788."

In 1993, the Mossman AOG erected a church on the Gorge Road, two kilometres from the mission at Gorge Reserve and mission. The Mossman Gazette reported Ps. Westbrook as saying

> Our new church building declares the faithful support of the committed people of this fellowship. There are some well-known and respected names, like Sister Hetherington, Pastor Davidson and Pastor Easton, who were among the early pioneers of this local fellowship. Today the church has expanded in vision to support missionaries in India, Sri Lanka and New Guinea, along with the Sunday School, Royal Rangers, youth camps and Christian education in all the schools in the shire.

The same year, the Commonwealth Native Title Act declared land available to Aboriginal claim, subject to conditions. The High Court finding of a title (the Mabo judgement over two small leases on Murray Island in Torres Strait) found just cause for Native Title in Common Law commensurate with that under Aboriginal law. The fact that Native Title rights predate European settlement are, as Longstaff (1997) notes "rights that we recognised but did not bestow. To replace them with legislated rights is to extinguish something original and replace it with something derived." The Cape York Aboriginal Land Council commissioned anthropologists to prepare claims under the authority of traditional owners.

BACK TO DAINTREE

In August 1995, the Mossman Assembly of God held a 'Back to Daintree Week', during which many former mission staff returned to pay homage to Isabella Hetherington. Research in the Mossman council records by Bill Fredericks located the site of her unmarked grave in the Mossman cemetery and Ps Valington Billy constructed a concrete tombstone which was dedicated at a gravesite service. Ps Westbrook said that "when Pastor Easton asked me to find Sister Hetherington's grave, the Council records simply gave a plot number and her name and recorded her as 'Missionary to Aboriginal people.' We went out and located the site and put a headstone on it."

Ps Jack Easton attended the gravesite dedication.

> It was through Sister Hetherington's preaching at the Canvas Cathedral that I was called. William Booth-Clibborns mother, the Marechealle, was a wonderful Evangelist. She was the daughter of William Booth. Evangeline was her name. Marechealle was the name given to her by the French. She was put in prison for preaching the Gospel and while she was there she wrote a wonderful hymn, 'Best Beloved of My Soul.' Wonderful words. I've memorized them all because I often sing them to myself. When people go through difficult times they've got nothing to cling to. I start singing some of these hymns. And this hymn she wrote in prison.
>
> *'Wicked men may persecute*
>
> *Banishing to solitude*
>
> *They should know my joy is Jesus*

Whom they never understood

At his voice my gloom disperses

Heavenly sunshine takes its place

Bars and bolts can not withhold him

Nor hide from me his lovely face.'

> When I went through hard and difficult times in my early years, I used to quote those words to myself, and they became a part of me and I entered into the experience that she had. It delivered me from the powers that would hold us captive. Hard times, difficult times, you'd sink down low. We got a lot of cheer from those words and the spirit of that hymn just gripped me.

At the end of 1995, the Brethren departed from the Mossman Gorge leaving only itinerant missionaries. At the time of writing, the Kuku-Yalanji, State and Local government authorities are considering how up to 30 parcels of vacant Crown land might be claimed under legislation. Aboriginal community development includes tourism employment and administration infrastructure. Hafner (1996:21) says that the Kuku-Yalanji "continue to assert their ownership… seeking a determination of their native title is one demonstration of their numerous and active links with the land." In 1998 the Cape York Health Council (Apunipima) identified alcohol "as the most pressing social problem facing Aboriginal communities" (Australian. 24/2/98:6).

A few kilometres up the road from the Gorge Community, the Mossman Assembly of God has begun to build a Retirement Village adjacent to the church. All that remains of the church at the former Daintree Mission is a concrete slab. The mission house burnt down some years ago and the present cane farm owner's house stands on the site. The dormitory is in an advanced state of disrepair and there is no access to the mission cemetery. The water pipes form part of a shed and coconut palms line the track while the Daintree river rolls by. The little church at the Gorge, built during the 1960's, stands beside the mission bell, a length of sugar-tram track which rings sweet when struck with the piece of water pipe that lies in the grass at the base of a large frangipanni tree (6).

ENDNOTES:

1. QSA - R254 - Box 750 6Q/2.
2. A description and defence of the A.I.M. (Australian Inland Mission) is given by its founder, the Rev. John Flynn (The 'Inlander' Jubilee Edition December 1971) in an interview shortly before his death in 1951. See also The Silent Heart. Griffiths, M. 1993:79. Kenthurst. S.A.: Kangaroo Press.
3. Ps. Jack Easton personal conversation. Brisbane. Dec. 1997.
4. The Evangel.' April 1982.
5. 'A River is Flowing.' The results of an AOG survey showed that at 1996, there were 244 AOG churches in Qld. 542 ordained ministers, 31,856 adherents and 4 state departments.
6. The AOG Mossman church was invited to hold a worship service at the Mossman Gorge Community Church on 14 March 1999.

Illustration 39. Assembly of God, Mossman Congregation, CWA Hall, 1989 (Mossman AOG collection).

Illustration 40. Missionaries Lillian Westbrook, Jack Goulder, Doug and Leila Gallienne, Jack Easton at Isobel Hetherington's grave, Mossman.

Illustration 41. Church at Mossman Gorge community 1997 (Mossman AOG collection).

REFERENCES

Anderson, J.C. 1979. Aboriginal Economy and Contact Relations at Bloomfield River, North Queensland. AIAS Newsletter 12: 33-37.

1984. The Political and Economic Basis of Kuku-Yalanji Social History. A thesis submitted in the Department of Anthropology and Sociology, University of Queensland, Australia, for the degree of Doctor of Philosophy.

1988. A Case Study in Failure: Kuku-Yalanji and the Lutherans at Bloomfield River, 1887 - 1902. Aboriginal Australians and Christian Missions, ed. Swain & Rose. Bedford Park, S.A.: Australian Association for the Study of Religions.

1989. Like a crane standing on one leg on a little island: an investigation of factors affecting the lifestyle of Wujalwujal community, North Queensland. Report to the National Aboriginal and Islander Legal Services Secretariat. Cited in Hafner, D. 1996.

1994. Wunbuwarra-Banana Creek Land Claim: The Kuku-Nyungkul Group. Documents prepared on behalf of the claimants. Cited in Hafner. 1996.

Antonios, Z. 1995. Alcohol Report: Racial Discrimination Act 1975. Canberra: Australian Government Printing Service.

ATSIC. 1998. As a Matter of Fact: The Myths and Misconceptions about Indigenous Australians. Woden: Office of Aboriginal Affairs.

Bamanga Bubu Ngadimunku. 1996. Aspects and Images: Kuku-Yalanji Life at Mossman Gorge. Mossman: Bamanga Bubu Ngadimunku Inc.

Beale, E. 1970. Kennedy of Cape York. Adelaide: Rigby.

Bennett, M. M. 1927. Christison of Lammermoor. London: Alston Rivers Ltd.

Berndt, Ronald & Catherine. 1988a. Body and Soul: More Than An Episode. Aboriginal Australians and Christian Missions. Ed. T. Swain & D. B. Rose. Bedford Park, S.A.: Australian Association for the Study of Religions.

Brennan, F. 1998. Land Rights -The Religious Factor (1993). Religious Business: Essays in Australian Aboriginal Spirituality. Ed. Charlesworth. Cambridge: CUP.

Brown, J. P. 1999. The Church - Bearing the Hurt of the Marginalized. International Review of Mission. Undated. Ref. # 9165. Institute for Aboriginal and Islander Studies. Canberra.

Buthman, T. 1997. Project Officer, Aboriginal and Torres Strait Islander Mental Health, Cairns. Notes from presentation to the Land and Spirit workshop. Psychosomatic Medicine Conference. Cairns. 7 page typescript.

Chant, B. 1973. Heart of Fire. S.A.: Luke Publications.

1997. The Hallowed Touch. Unpublished manuscript. Sydney: Tabor College.

1998. Isabella Hetherington. Unpublished manuscript. Sydney: Tabor College.

d'Abbs, P. et al. 1994. Alcohol Misuse and Violence: Alcohol-related Violence in Aboriginal and Torres Strait Islander Communities: a Literature Review. Canberra: Commonwealth Information Services.

Docker, E. 1970. The Blackbirders. Sydney: Angus & Robertson.

Erbacher, J & S. 1991. Aborigines of the Rainforest: Survival in the Rainforest. Cambridge: University Press.

Evans, K. 1969. Missionary Effort Towards The Cape York Aborigines, 1886 -1910: A Study of Culture Contact. University of Queensland: Unpublished Thesis. B A with Hons.

Farnfield, J. 1968. Frontiersman: A biography of George Elphinstone Dalrymple. Melbourne: Oxford University Press.

Franken, F. 1964. Mowbray River and Port Douglas. Cairns Historical Society. Bulletin No. 61. March.

Gondarra, D. 1993. Pentecost in Arnhem Land. Renewal Journal. Vol 1. No. 1. GPO Box 674. Brisbane. 4001.

1996. The Australian. 18th October.

Green, N. 1996. The Mission as a Total Institution: Forrest River Mission under Ernest Gribble. Lectures in North Qld History. Townsville: JCU.

Guy, R. 1999. Baptised Among Crocodiles: A Contact History and Social Science Perspective of the Daintree Aboriginal Mission 1940 -1962. A thesis submitted in the Department of Psychology and Sociology, James Cook University for the degree of Master of Social Science.

Hafner, D. 1996. A Sketch History of the Eastern Kuku-Yalanji and Their Region. Diane Hafner, 56 Waverley Rd. Camp Hill. Qld. 23 page typescript. Unpublished. Undated. The work quotes a reference at 1995 and was cited by the author in 1996.

Hasluck, P. 1988. Shades of Darkness: Aboriginal Affairs 1925-1965. Carlton: Melbourne University Press.

Harris, J. 1990. One Blood - 200 years of Aboriginal Contact with Christianity. Sydney: Albatross Books.

Harrison, J. 1990. Mapoon: The Early Years. Journey. October. AIATSIS bibl. 1993. ref: 635.

Haviland, J. & L. 1980. How Much Food Will There Be In Heaven: Lutherans and Aborigines Around Cooktown to 1900. Aboriginal History. 4 (2). AIATSIS 1980-81 bibl. Ref: 424.

Haviland, J. B. & Hart, R. 1998. Old Man Fog and the Last Aborigines of Barrow Point. Bathurst: Crawford Publishing House.

Herschberger, H. & R. 1964. Aboriginal Institute for Aboriginal Languages. Canberra.

Higgins, G. 1981. James Noble of Yarrabah. Missions Publications of Australia: Lawson, N.S.W.

Howitt, R. 1998. Defiant struggle for reparation. The Australian. 26/3/98:13.

Hunt. S. 1978. Assemblies of God: story of its foundation and mission. Sydney: Assembly Press.

Hunter, E. 1993. Aboriginal Health and History: power and prejudice in remote Australia. New York: Cambridge University Press.

Hunter et al. 1999. An Analysis of Suicide in Indigenous Communities of North Queensland: The Historical, Cultural and Symbolic Landscape. Ernest Hunter, Joseph Reser, Mercy Baird, Paul Reser. Cairns: University of Queensland, Department of Social and Preventive Medicine.

Jakalbaku. 1988. The Douglas Shire Council Bi-Centenary Committee. Ed. Denis Field with contributions from Kuku-Yalanji.. Personal interview with Wilma Walker of Mossman.

Johnston, W. T. & J. Cairns. 1986. Port Douglas: a history sketch record. P.O. Box 410 Atherton. 4883.

Jones, P. 1988. Dreamings. Ed. Peter Sutton. New York: Viking.

Kerr. J. 1979. Northern Outpost. Mossman, Qld: Mossman Central Mill.

Kirkman, N. 1980. The Palmer River Goldfield. Lectures in North Queensland history, vol. 1. Edited by K.H. Kennedy. Townsville: James Cook University.

Kunoth-Monks, R. 1987. Church and Culture: An Aboriginal Perspective. The Gospel is not Western. Ed. G. Trompf. New York: Orbis Books.

Lake, M. The Australian. 3/6/97.

Longstaff, S. 1997. Executive Director, St. James Ethics Centre, Sydney. Australian. 1/12/97. p. 13.

Loos, N. 1982. Invasion and Resistance - Aboriginal-European Relations on the North Queensland Frontier 1861 -1897. ANU Press, Canberra.

1988. Concern and Contempt: Church and missionary Attitudes Towards Aborigines in North Queensland in the Nineteenth Century. Aboriginal Australians and Church Missions. Ed. Swain and Rose. Netley, S.A: Australian Association for the Study of Religions.

Lloyd, B. 1994. A Walk back into the history of Port Douglas 1877-1994. Port Douglas Historical Society.

1997. A Walk on the Waterfront: Port Douglas 1877 to the Present. Port Douglas Historical Society.

Manne, R. 1998. The Stolen Generations. Quadrant. Jan/Feb. pp. 53-63.

McDonald. 1997. Australian Review of Books. December.

McGregor, E. 1997. Imagined Destinies: Aboriginal Australians and the Doomed Race Theory, 1880 -1939. Melbourne: MUP.

1997b. Cited in JCU Outlook, p. 4. Townsville: James Cook University.

Meston, A. 1896. Report on the Aborigines of Queensland to the Home Secretary. Qld Parliament. Votes and Proceedings 4:723 - 740.

Morgan, M. 1985. A Drop in the Bucket. Box Hill, Victoria: United Aborigines Mission.

Mitchell, N. 1996. Interview with the author at Fred Leftwich Retirement Home, Mareeba. Queensland. 6/2/96.

Niau, J. 1936. The Phantom Paradise. Sydney: Angus & Robertson.

Nielsen, L. 1997. Daintree: jewel of tropical North Queensland, pub. Nielsen. Mt Molloy. Qld.

Pearson, G. 1997. Health and Land go Hand in Hand. Speech given at the Land, Body and Spirit Workshop. 14th World Congress of Psychosomatic Medicine, Cairns. September. Copy in possession of author.

Pike, G. 1978. Northern Frontier. Sydney: Rigby.

QSA. Queensland State Archives. Accessed through the Department of Families, Youth and Community Care. Brisbane.

Read, P. 1998. All for One, One for All. Australian Review of Books. July.

Reser & Eastwell. 1981. Labelling and Cultural Expectations: The Shaping of a Sorcery Syndrome in Aboriginal Australia. Journal of Nervous and Mental Disease. Vol. 169. #5.

Reser, J.P. 1990. A perspective on the causes and cultural context of violence in Aboriginal communities in North Queensland. Report to the Royal Commission into Aboriginal Deaths in Custody.

Roth, W. E. 1900. A Report to the Under-Secretary from the Northern Protector of Aboriginals. Votes and Proceedings. 5.584. Queensland State Archives.

Rowley, C.D. 1972. The Destruction of Aboriginal Society. Sydney: Halstead Press.

Rowse, T. 1993. After Mabo; Interpreting Indigenous Traditions. Melbourne: University Press.

Scherer, P.A. 1973. From Joiner's Bench to Pulpit. Adelaide: Lutheran Publishing House.

Smith, D & G. 1987. Rivers Are Flowing. Melbourne: Assembly of God.

Thompson, D. 1982. Bora is like Church. Sydney: The Australian Board of Missions.

1996. Struggling for Relevance at Lockhardt River. Lectures in North Queensland History. Townsville: James Cook University.

Trigger, D. S. 1992. Whitefella' Comin'. Cambridge, UK.: University Press.

Vale, E. 1948. Letter to the Director of Native Affairs. Brisbane. QSA. February 10th, 1948.

Warner, W. L. 1937. A Black Civilisation. Massachusetts: Harper & Row.

Warby. J. 1996. The Lockhardt Catalyst. Lectures in North Qld History. Townsville: JCU.

Wells, E. 1982. Reward and Punishment in Arnhem land 1962 -1963. Canberra: Australian Institute of Aboriginal Studies.

Wood, R. 1990. Aboriginal Interests in Port Douglas and Environs. A report to Environment Science and Services. P.O. Box 107. Spring Hill. 4004. Queensland.